DATE DUE

AUG 0 6 1999	NOV 3 2005
	MAR 2 0 2006
DEC 15 1999	
NOV 0 6 2001	
NOV 2 6 2001	
SEP 2 4 2003	
7-7-04	
NOV 2 9 2004	

GAYLORD M

Raising Sons
Without Fathers

Raising Sons Without Fathers

◆ ◆ ◆ ◆ ◆

A Woman's Guide to Parenting Strong, Successful Boys

Leif G. Terdal, Ph.D.,
and Patricia Kennedy

A BIRCH LANE PRESS BOOK
Published by Carol Publishing Group

KVCC KALAMAZOO VALLEY
COMMUNITY COLLEGE
LIBRARY

To the mothers and sons of America

A Birch Lane Press Book
Published by Carol Publishing Group
Birch Lane Press is a registered trademark of Carol Communications, Inc.

Editorial, sales and distribution, rights and permissions inquiries should be addressed to Carol Publishing Group, 120 Enterprise Avenue, Secaucus, N.J. 07094

In Canada: Canadian Manda Group, One Atlantic Avenue, Suite 105, Toronto, Ontario, M6K 3E7

Carol Publishing Group books may be purchased in bulk at special discounts for sales promotion, fund-raising, or educational purposes. Special editions can be created to specifications. For details, contact Special Sales Department, 120 Enterprise Avenue, Secaucus, N.J. 07094.

Manufactured in the United States of America
10   9   8   7   6   5   4   3   2   1

Library of Congress Cataloging-in-Publication Data

Terdal, Leif G., 1937–
    Raising sons without fathers : a woman's guide to parenting strong, successful boys / Leif Terdal and Patricia Kennedy.
        p.   cm.
    ISBN 1-55972-342-4 (hardcover)
    1. Children of single parents.   2. Mothers and sons.   3. Single mothers.   4. Paternal deprivation.   5. Child rearing.   I. Kennedy, Patricia, 1949—
HQ774.4.T47   1996
649′.132—dc20   95-47098
                                                                CIP

Contents

◆ ◆ ◆ ◆ ◆

Acknowledgments

◆ ◆ ◆ ◆ ◆

We appreciate the support and input from clinicians who work with families and provided critical comments, expertise, time, and interest. Barbara Dworschak, Jan Goldman, Dr. John Hale, Nancy Madian, Ellie Moe, Dr. Virginia Silvey, Morgan Dickerson, Laura Foley, Kelly Grimes, Abby Terris, and Susan R. Nelson.

Extraordinary thanks go to Dr. Eric J. Mash and Dr. Judith Barker for sharing their special expertise. Paul Terdal and Tim Kennedy deserve special thanks for their technical assistance, as do Marg Petersen and Linda Varsell Smith.

We also wish to thank the mothers, fathers, and sons who shared their personal stories with us. They shaped the material and structure of this book.

Preface

♦ ♦ ♦ ♦ ♦

You've heard the statistics, and you've seen the talk shows. More and more children are growing up in single-parent homes. If current estimates prove true, one of every two children born after 1975 will spend at least some of his youth in a single-parent home. Discussing the problems isn't enough—parents want answers. What can they do to help their sons grow up as strong, well-adjusted young men in a single-parent home? This book is designed to help you, the mother, and your son through the fatherless period.

Children, of course, are strongly influenced by their family. It may be better for a child to live in a single-parent home than in a two-parent family with continuous conflict and arguments. All children feel stress when the family deals with divorce or death of a parent. However, boys express their problems differently than girls do. A young girl who is stressed may develop low self-esteem or depression. While boys also experience low self-esteem and depression, they rarely admit it. Their behavior is likely to be misunderstood, and they are more likely to misunderstand what it means to a man. They may mistake aggression for normal masculine behavior; they may even find male companionship and understanding in a gang. Of the men in prison, many were once stressed young men from single-parent homes. The numbers of young men raised in single-parent homes is rising, and the problem is growing in middle-class America. For all of these reasons, this book focuses on boys from single-parent families.

Single mothers want answers and help. This book is aimed at helping you find those answers by looking at your problems from various, sometimes less obvious perspectives. It offers ideas, suggestions, and possibilities for the many hurdles single mothers face—from telling your child about divorce, to time management and financial difficulties. For your convenience, we have included a long list of resources in the appendix. You are not alone in your journey, and there is help along the way.

I

♦ ♦ ♦ ♦ ♦

Sons Without Fathers
The Problems They Face

1

Sons at Risk

There is no question that the Dan Quayle—*Murphy Brown* controversy opened up discussion on the importance of fathers in families. Research on fatherless families is abundant, and it indicates that the children in these families are at risk, especially the sons. Fatherless children, boys particularly, are less likely to finish high school, more likely to suffer emotionally and economically, and more likely to have difficulty forming relationships.

At a time when fatherless sons struggle to master the tasks of growing up in a changing and more complex world, they must do so with seriously weakened family support. As family support weakens, these children and their families face reductions in access to publicly supported programs in health, education and human services. It is our view that these difficult and overlapping problems make boys—our sons—particularly vulnerable.

Problems Faced by Fatherless Children

Today many marriages end in divorce, and too often the children in broken families face continued exposure to ongoing conflict between their parents.[1] In the majority of these families, the father's role is diminished or ineffective.[2] Without a father in the

3

home to model male behavior and demonstrate the positive role fathers play, boys often develop an inadequate understanding of what it means to be a man.

Divorce is not the only way boys are deprived of a father. While divorce or a father's death causes trauma in his son's life, perhaps a more tragic situation is never knowing a father's love, protection, or example within a family setting. Since 1964 the number of out-of-wedlock births to women under the age of twenty has continued to rise.[3] Children in these families are at greater risk to be born to a mother who did not obtain adequate prenatal care and are more likely to have a low birthweight and delays in their development.[4]

When a family is fatherless, it is more likely to become poor, even if it started out with a middle-class or upper-class income, and increasingly, in our society, single women and their children make up the highest percentage of the poor.[5] Also child abuse in the forms of physical abuse, neglect, emotional abuse, or sexual abuse continues.[6]

Boys raised in fatherless homes with multiple problems often do not complete their schooling,[7] commit crimes that bring them into the juvenile court system,[8] and carry inadequate parenting into the next generation.

A Look at the Issues

For many generations the United States has been a symbol of great opportunity and substantial individual freedoms. As a nation we have tremendous natural resources and a productive and developing industrial base. Our public and private universities are the finest in the world. Yet many of our children are at a disadvantage because their families do not provide effective guidance and support during their childhood. America does not seem to have committed itself to its children. This book is written for parents—mothers and fathers—who face difficult choices in their lives, and for the children who are affected by those choices.

We have organized a broad array of issues around the perspectives of sons, mothers, and fathers caught in the struggle of life without fathers. We have made a number of recommendations in this book. They are for your consideration and discussion within your family and circle of friends. We think that in the best of all worlds couples would not have a child until they have had a stable and committed relationship for five years. But parents must deal not with what should be but with what is. The children are here now, and in many cases in less than perfect situations. Our book focuses on ways to deal with sons who are without a father, for whatever period of time.

Communication: Telling Children About Divorce

For now, lets start with very basic communication—how a child learns that his family (that is, his world) will change. Let's look at how some boys learn that they are about to be raised without a father living in the home. There are myriad issues that we all need to think about. How the child is told of a family breakup is important, which presents challenges for the mother, the father, and the son.

John

This is how John, age nine, and his older sister were told that their parents were going to get a divorce: John's father had recently returned home from a month-long trip, which was actually a trial separation. This time when dad came home there were no arguments between him and John's mother. Together they planned an evening barbecue with hamburgers, potato chips, soda and ice cream. They were smiling and getting along. John knew his mother and father had some major problems, but he thought that his parents were putting on a family picnic like they used to do when things were going well.

Then Dad said, "Your mother and I want each of you to know that we are going to get a divorce. We just are not able to get along together. The two of you will live here at the house with Mom. I'll live in an apartment somewhere else. I'll work out visitations with you."

John was stunned. Frequently children are upset and confused when their parents divorce. Although most children are good observers, many need help with interpretation. John had expected his parents to try to work things out. That expectation was reinforced by the pleasantries of the barbecue. Now he had to deal with both the very difficult news of the divorce as well as being confused by the way he learned about it.

Much later John was able to understand that his parents had worked through their anger over continuing problems. For them the decision to divorce, as difficult as it was, eased their pain.

Steven

This is how Steven heard about divorce in his family: Steven's mother and father argued often, and on two occasions his father struck his mother. One day, in the heat of an argument between his parents, the father yelled to his son, "Your mother doesn't want me to live here anymore," and with that he stormed out of the house.

Steven, at age seven, was left frightened, confused, and angry.

Michael

Michael had come to his pediatrician for a well-child exam and was accompanied by his grandmother. In an effort to put Michael at ease, the doctor asked him, "Michael, who lives at home with you?"

Michael replied, "My mother and my father."

His grandmother, sitting behind him, shook her head no. When she found a moment to speak privately with the pediatrician, she told him that Michael had lived with her for the past three years and had not seen his father during that time, and his mother had seen him only infrequently. The boy's father had never participated in rearing Michael, and the mother had withdrawn from parenting over the past three years. While the grandmother was the effective parent, the arrangement had not been formalized. Her daughter could come at any time to take Michael back and she, the grandmother, feared that would happen. She also knew that her daughter was incapable of being a good parent. Michael was one step away from foster care. If his grandmother had not stepped in to help and provide care, Michael would have been placed in a foster home.

Better Ways to Tell Children About Divorce

Understanding is the first step for a child in dealing with a major change in his family. The child must be aware of, acknowledge, and comprehend the change, whether it results from death, divorce, or desertion. But what a child must know may be difficult for adults to communicate. We create problems for children when we present information that misrepresents or obscures the facts.

Adjusting to Divorce

John

To evaluate how these three children came to know about a change in their family situation: John's family handled it best. Both his parents were present, and both participated in talking to their children. They reviewed what they were going to say and how they would say it, and they were civil to each other. They told their son he would live with his mother and that his father would maintain a relationship with him. The fact that John was visibly upset is understandable because divorce is hard for children. He had hoped that his parents would not split up. However, the party atmosphere obscured the news and made it hard for him to express his grief and disappointment. It is sometimes particularly difficult for boys to express sadness; how he heard the news made it even harder.

Steven

Steven's situation was far more difficult. His parents did not work out a plan for how they would tell him. His father was very angry and blamed his wife for his having to leave the family: "Your mother doesn't want me to live here anymore!" Other than telling him he was leaving, the father did not explain to Steven who would care for him or whether he would maintain a relationship with him.

Michael

Michael's situation was even more trying, because confusion is worse than error. A child should not have to figure out his family's circumstances. Michael had not been told that his parents were divorced, nor had he been told that his grandmother would be his parent. Because he was not told that his mother and father would not be raising him, he could not begin to accept the situation. Not only did he reject it emotionally, he did not understand it. The grandmother played an important role for Michael, but the ambiguous and unspoken arrangement made it hard for her and Michael as well. His mother's failure to communicate with Michael and with her own mother reflected a serious inability to cope.

Understanding Divorce

Children need clear information about an impending divorce, and it is better if both parents are present and can handle the discussion without becoming emotionally heated. They can skip details of the problems that led to their divorce; children need and want to know how it will affect them. They should be told who will care for them, what their living arrangements will be, and how visitation will work. They need to know that their parents are divorcing each other, not them, and that their family will still exist, but it will be different.

Children may not understand some things about a divorce for years afterwards. For example, some children worry and wonder if they somehow caused the divorce. They may believe that if they were better behaved, or smarter, or more lovable, then surely their parents would not want to live apart. A child can carry guilt over "causing" a divorce for years. It takes time and maturity to resolve this, and simple reassurance seldom heals the wound.

When your family unit is changed by divorce or death, you know it is going to change your child's world. Children need to understand and accept the permanance of divorce, which also takes time. It helps for both parents to be sensitive, loving, and patient with their children as they adjust to the divorce. Divorce changed the lives of John and Steven.

After the Divorce: John

Initially John was troubled and upset by his parents' divorce. However, a lot of factors in his life remained stable and secure. He continued to live in the same house with his mother and sister. He kept his neighborhood friends, and he attended the same school. His father visited on a regular basis and maintained a close relationship with him and his sister. Despite the financial strains the divorce created, John's father made his child support payments and helped out financially when unexpected costs arose. Both sets of grandparents saw the children regularly. John should experience an emotionally stable and happy childhood.

His parents' divorce did not break the important contract with him; they maintained an active commitment to both of their children.

After the Divorce: Steven

Steven's situation presented more difficulties after the divorce as well. He was told of the pending divorce in a way that was most upsetting to him. His father's angry shout, "Your mother doesn't want me living here anymore!" was painful for him.

While we were concerned about how Steven was told of the divorce, we were also concerned about the other issues he faced. His father did not make arrangements to pay child support, and his mother was anxious and indecisive about putting legal pressure on her former spouse. For financial reasons, she was forced to move to a lower-rent neighborhood, so Steven lost contact with his old friends. With all that was going on in his life he was too distressed and uncomfortable to make new friends. His mother was so busy with her new job and managing on her own that she had little time to meet neighbors or make new friends, and before long she lost touch with her old friends as well.

Steven's mother was too upset and preoccupied to become acquainted with her son's new teacher. She failed to monitor her son's schoolwork. His father visited only sporadically and infrequently, and acted as if *he* were the victim of the failed marriage. Steven also lost contact with his grandparents. Alone and isolated, he turned into an angry boy.

For Steven, the divorce compounded his problems because his father was unwilling or unable to maintain the role of a parent. Steven was not born "out of wedlock" or "with a broken promise," but the result was the same. He was raised with a broken promise because his father was no longer a responsible parent.

Other Scenarios

The three cases we looked at were the result of divorce. Some children are born to women who are not married at the time of conception and birth, while others experience the death of a parent. A father's death presents a different set of problems for both a mother and son.

Death of a Father

Twelve-year-old Robert was the oldest of six children—four brothers and two sisters. His father worked on an assembly line and repaired cars on the side to make extra money. His mother was a full-time homemaker and cared for her children, handled family finances, and was active in the community through churchwork and volunteer efforts. At age twelve Robert's world suddenly fell in on him. His father, who had been healthy, became ill. At first the doctors thought he had an ulcer, but his condition worsened. Within months he became incapacitated and could no longer work. After a brief hospitalization he died, and it was determined he had a rapidly developing form of stomach cancer.

The death was a shock to the family and changed many things. Its source of income was lost, as well as the father's help and guidance in raising the children. In response to the crisis, family members on both sides offered continued assistance even long after the funeral. Family members who lived far away sent clothing for the children and money to assist with expenses, and those nearby made certain the family had food and helped with immediate needs. Also, church members offered help, condolence, and support.

All four sons and the two daughters went on to complete school, form committed relationships, earn a living, and contribute to society. It was not done easily. Some years after his dad's death, Robert would still be reminded of his father and develop feelings of intense sadness. Each of the children mourned the death in somewhat different ways, in part depending on their age. After the funeral the youngest boy, who was two years old, asked when his dad was coming home. He did not understand the finality of the death until about six months later. As is so often the case, the mother mourned the death for a considerable period of time, but she went on with the business of raising her children.

The Single Parent Who Adopts

Adoption also can lead to families without a father. Adel Palmer was single and did not plan to marry, but she wanted to be a parent. She worked as a nurse and felt that she had the personal resources to be an effective parent, and she had friends and family who supported her idea and would help out with some aspects of child care, as needed. She is now raising two adopted children and is successfully meeting their financial and emotional needs.

Children Born Out of Wedlock

About five hundred thousand teenage girls give birth each year.[9] Some tell us, "It is seldom an accident. You know what you're doing—having unprotected sex." One said, "When I was younger, nobody loved me, and I thought my baby would always love me and never walk out on me." Another offered, "My boyfriend wanted me to have a child—for him." Still another mother told us, "I don't need a man. It's a baby I want. Besides, I have a grown brother, and I will have boyfriends."

When we look at the children of those young women we find some may feel differently. Let's contrast the comments of these young mothers with the thoughts of a young man who grew up without a stable and nurturing father in the home. His "father figures" consisted of a series of men who had mostly transient relationships with his mother. In his book, *Out of the Madness* Jerrold Ladd wrote:[10]

> But I despised every man that came over to take advantage of my poor mother. I let them know it, too, through looks, snarls, frowns, and much later with fists and knives. The ones who stayed awhile, some weeks, some months, earned respect. Most of the time, though, the men would not stay. This meant that there constantly was a different man as a father in our lives. You can imagine how confused we became as children. The minute we adapted to the new one, he was replaced by another one....[11]
>
> But other men, I learned in 1978, were out just to take advantage of a weak, unschooled woman. It didn't matter, though; every new man she had we called Daddy. That's how bad we longed for a father figure, then, at our young ages. None of them was worth a damn. Some of them I despised. One of them, _____, hit her, a woman, in the face.[12]

Baby Born Out of Wedlock—or—With a Broken Promise

The expression "out of wedlock" has been criticized for being derogatory. But the expression itself does not begin to communicate the hazards associated with such a vulnerable birth. A more accurate expression would be "with a broken promise." The implied understanding is that at birth a child will have two parents committed to his well-being throughout their lives. The promise is broken if one parent voluntarily no longer acts as one, or if one forces the other out of the parenting role. Either way, the great majority of children born "out of wedlock" pass through their childhood without the active and nurturing role of both a mother and a father. We can not stress strongly enough the point that a baby born "with a broken promise" indeed has a problem, but it is not of his or her doing.

Baby Born With a Broken Promise—Adult Style

Most children born, as we say, "with a broken promise" are not a result of a teenage pregnancy. About 70 percent of unmarried mothers are over twenty years old,[13] and some women risk pregnancy by having unprotected sex with a partner in the apparent hope that their relationship will improve.

Martha

Martha had an affair with a married man with children and became pregnant. Her companion would not leave his marriage, and she decided to keep the paternity of her child secret to avoid embarrassment for herself and her "partner." He agreed, informally, to help her out financially—when he "could."

Susan

Susan had an affair with several men concurrently. When she became pregnant she realized that the father was a small player in her life. She did not have a close relationship with him and did not want him to be part of her life as she prepared to raise her child. The youngster's father did not know that his brief encounter resulted in a pregnancy, so he had no involvement in the upbringing of his son. Susan's child is another youngster born "with a broken promise."

Out of Wedlock—or—Motherhood in the Absence of a Suitable Partner

Lisa

Lisa is attractive, well educated and is launched on a financially rewarding career track. When she was a college student her long-term goals were to pursue a career, get married, and have children. Except for maternity leaves, she planned to continue working throughout her parenting years. She also had some basic criteria and expectations of the man she would marry. She wanted one who would:

- respect and encourage her in her career efforts, but would not be intimidated by them
- have a strong commitment to career goals himself
- be committed to raising children in a healthy and supportive family
- handle disagreements and conflicts within the relationship through communication rather than intimidation and threats
- share a mutual attraction and affection as a basis for a developing relationship

Now, at age thirty-three, Lisa is a single parent raising a four-year-old son, Mark. Lisa has not married, and although she is open to marriage she is not optimistic it will occur. When we asked her about the birth of her son and the relationship that led to her pregnancy, she said, "While I had planned to marry and raise a family, I did not need to marry for financial security."

She added, "My relationships with men were a major disappointment. First of all, a number of men seemed taken aback that my career would put me on a higher salary scale than theirs. I did not expect or insist that my future husband would have to earn more money than me, but a lot of men seemed bothered that I would likely earn more than them.

"I am not alone in this. A friend of mine is an African-American fourth-year medical student. She told me that in the Pacific Northwest, where she is doing her studies, she does not think there is a single, black, eligible male. She mentioned that on the few dates she had had, the guy shuts down when she says [in answer to a question about career plans] that she is earning an M.D. degree and plans to practice medicine.

"In addition, a lot of the young men I have dated don't seem to be on track for a significant career. Some don't seem to have a clue about the economy or what it takes to succeed in today's world."

Lisa had been disturbed by the attitudes and behaviors of some of the men about issues of equality and how they handled disagreements. She insisted that she didn't want a marriage if it would be a continuing problem and disappointment, but she very much wanted to raise a child. She met a young man—in his thirties—Ph.D. research scientist at a university in California. He met some of her criteria but not all. For one, he was not willing to commit to a long-term relationship. But she did enter an intimate relationship with him and conceived a child. She is now raising their son independently, and there is very little contact between Mark and his father.

Lisa bought a house and is able to afford child care. She enjoys attending the symphony and other cultural activities despite her busy schedule. She has a number of friends, including some with young children who play with Mark. She expresses confidence that she will continue to be an effective parent for her son.

We asked her if being an unmarried woman—and a mother— has caused problems for her. "Well," she said, "I might be viewed as a morally unstable person, but I am willing to deal with that."

She made a point of saying she had a very real problem: She had to decide whether she would give up her chance in life to be a mother and raise a child or enter a marriage that she knew from the beginning probably would not work. Her decision to have her child was not an easy one.

"I know there are men out there who would be suitable for me. Some are already married—and I view them as off limits. I simply did not find a suitable man to marry."

Diverse Families

Earlier we had suggested substituting child born "with a broken promise" for "out of wedlock," in Lisa's situation her pregnancy was not the result of a casual encounter. Not only was the pregnancy planned, but she thought of herself as a prospective mother and was financially and emotionally prepared to raise a child alone. Her situation brings up a question many women consider: whether or not the pool of eligible men who are responsible and ready to commit to a marital relationship is sufficient for women of today.

While the answer may well be that not enough men are available for professional women with ticking biological time clocks, we ask all women to give equal weight to the emotional needs of the child in balancing their desire for motherhood. The child's emotional welfare is as important as the mother's and deserves equal consideration. Many women feel they do not need a husband or a father for their child, and it is difficult to convince well-educated mature women, let alone teenage girls, that a son without a father is at a disadvantage.

Committed Relationship, Outside Legal Marriage

In this age of diversity, many children are born into families that are not legally recognized by church or state. While children may be born "out of wedlock," they are not necessarily born "out of promise." If both parents are committed to the family and the child's needs throughout life, and if the relationship is stable, then the youngster will not share the risk factors of children born "with a broken promise."

Mary and John

Mary and John have been together for the past seven years. They get along well and are successful in their careers. They share a house, a car, and household furniture. Mary would like to marry John and raise a family. John wanted to continue living with Mary but didn't want to get married. He was faithful to her, they planned a pregnancy together, and she gave birth to a healthy boy. While their child was born "out of wedlock," the child was not born "out of promise." The child has a mother and a father, both of whom are committed to family life in which the child's needs come first.

Each scenario offers a different twist on how things play out for children and their families. It is our hope in writing this book that we do not fall into the trap of minimizing the very realistic problems faced by some children who are raised without a father's presence in the home. We also do not want to make a list of simple solutions that might not work even if faithfully carried out. Finally, we do not want to imply that single parenting is always harmful to children.

We do wish to acknowledge the broad spectrum of issues that contribute to a child's development. While we will use examples, we share them not to tell horror stories but to present ideas and information that can be helpful to mothers, fathers, and their children.

2

Problems and Solutions

Single mothers tell us that lone parenting brings up four issues: money problems, work overload, loss of contact with friends, and arguments with the former spouse.

Money Problems

Mothers raising children as single parents have the highest poverty rate in the United States. According to McLanahan and Booth (1989), fully one-half of families in which the mother is a single parent are living below the poverty line.[1] In contrast, of two-parent families, just one in ten lives below the poverty line. Many of these families become poor following a divorce, so low income becomes a new and additional problem for the mother and her children.[2] In fact, women in high income brackets prior to divorce suffer the biggest decline in income.[3]

Why are middle-class and upper-middle-class women hurt economically by divorce? There are several reasons women are at an economic disadvantage relative to men. Some of these existed during the marriage but may not have been recognized by either partner. Others reflect unwieldy divorce settlements that do not take children's needs into account.

Should a divorce eventually occur the mother, not the father, is placed at an economic disadvantage by marriage because of several factors:[4]

1. Women are more involved with their children and assume greater responsibility for their family's domestic needs. Their time and focus is on family, not careers, in the early years of the marriage, when they are more likely to bear children. Many couples place a high priority on the husband's work, investing time and money in his career, education, and training. During this critical time the woman's career goals are "on hold," making professional advancement difficult.

2. Women earn less than men, and marriage increases the economic gap. Married men earn more than single men, whereas married women earn less than single women. In general, while men earn more than women (women's wages are about 70 percent of men's), on average married women earn only 50 percent as much as married men.

3. Divorce settlements are structured to provide a "clean break," with no obligation from one spouse to another. If a woman was a primary homemaker for an extended period of time, the courts still expect her to become self-sufficient in a short time, as though she had remained on a career track since college. Usually, she is not compensated for her efforts in assisting her husband start his career.

4. Child support payments depend on establishing paternity and awarding "child support orders," but usually support awards are insufficient to cover the costs of raising a child and do not cover college costs or university education. Even when awards are ordered, often the payments are not made, which means most women and their children face a relentless economic crisis following a divorce. This includes women who previously experienced middle-class financial security.

Lower Wages in the United States

Mothers raising children alone show the highest levels of poverty in the United States. During the past forty years the situation has worsened, both in numbers and degree. More women in the United States now raise children as single parents and do so with reduced income. According to an extensive report prepared by the Annie E. Casey Foundation in 1994, nineteen million, or 24 percent of America's children, live in families without a father present. In 1950, 6 percent of the children in the United States were living in families without a father. Of children born in the 1980s and beyond, about one-half will probably will live in a family without the father present.[5] As the number of fatherless families has increased the earning power of women has declined, when adjusted for inflation, except for those with college degrees or graduate school. According to information from the Bureau of Labor Statistics, the income of women who dropped out of or finished high school (when averaged) declined from 1979 to 1994. Women with college degrees, and advanced degrees, showed an increase in real earnings even after adjustments for inflation.

The Low U.S. Minimum Wage

Today the minimum wage in the United States of $4.25 an hour is at an all-time low and lower than current wage scales in Western Europe. In 1950 the minimum wage of workers in the United States was equal to 59 percent of the hourly pay of workers in nonsupervisory positions. In 1968 the minimum wage remained at a level equal to 58 percent of the pay of average hourly earnings, and it has been on a downward spiral ever since. By January 1978 it was 48 percent of average hourly earnings. In June 1995 the minimum wage of $4.25 represented just 37 percent of the average hourly wage in the United States.[7]

Without exception, the base wages in Western Europe are higher than in the United States. In European countries wages are set through collective bargaining agreements that are accepted industry-wide. These are monitored by the U.S. Department of Labor through the Office of Productivity and Technology.

How does the U.S. minimum wage compare with that of other developed nations? We have reviewed the minimum wages in the following European countries: Austria, Belgium, England, Denmark, Finland, France, Germany, Iceland, Ireland, Italy, the Netherlands, Sweden, and Switzerland. All have higher minimum wages than the United States. In Denmark the lowest wage at the end of 1994 was 68 kroner (U.S. $11.00) per hour, which is sufficient for an adequate standard of living for a worker and family.[8] In Ireland, a poor country by our standards, low-income families are entitled to additional benefits, such as subsidized housing and children's allowances.

A low minimum wage affect women and their children because women are likely to earn less than men. In Sweden the average hourly wage for women is 90 percent of the average earnings of men. Similar differences are found in Norway, Denmark, France, and the Netherlands. In the United States the average pay for women is about 70 percent of the average for men.[9]

Women and their children are especially hurt by existing wage scales in the United States. The historically low U.S. minimum wage equals an annual pay of $8,840, which is $3,350 below the estimated poverty level for a family of three[10]—insufficient to provide an adequate living.

Minimum-wage workers in the United States are predominately adults over the age of twenty, not teenagers, and 62 percent are women. A significant raise in the minimum wage would benefit other workers who earn just above it. For women who are single parents, even those who once enjoyed a middle-class lifestyle, declining wages at the low end of wage scales creates economic hardship.

Maternity and Parental Leave

European countries support families through paid maternity and parental leave. In Sweden a woman receives 90 percent of her pay for twelve weeks as a maternity benefit and qualifies for social security benefits for one year of parental leave.[11] Both of these measures support a family in raising a young child. The United States has a law that prohibits employment discrimination based on pregnancy and childbirth, but it does not have a national policy on maternity or parental leave.

Universal Health Support

European countries also provide universal health care, and this includes ongoing follow-up or well-baby care. Parents of infants and young children can also get information about child development, health, nutrition, and child behavior from child care workers. In Sweden and Scotland these are handled through home visits.

One Woman's Struggle and Success

Nicole was twenty-seven, with a one-year-old son, when her marriage ended. Prior to the divorce her husband had completed training for a profession and was at the start of a successful career. In contrast Nicole, who had only worked as a waitress, was left with major financial problems and a baby to raise.

She said, "I decided to go to college and find a way to earn enough to support myself and my son. I originally intended to become a medical technologist but discovered sociology along the way and ended up in graduate school. I want to emphasize that without the funding for child care, and other things, that existed at the time, I would still be in low-income jobs or on welfare."

Nicole was clearly not alone in facing a major financial problem following her divorce. She recognized that poverty would add a great deal of stress to parenting a child alone.

Nicole continued, "A real problem for most single parents, in my opinion, is poverty. It's hard to be a good parent in the midst of poverty. I was lucky because I found cheap affordable housing in a community of single parents, was able to go to college, and become upwardly mobile. I was able to combine school and motherhood in such a way that I could do both well—meaning I had faculty in my department who understood and supported parenting. However, I owed sixty thousand dollars in student loans when I finished. While others are buying homes and investing in retirement, I have these loans to pay off. I will have bills all my life. That's the debt I have to pay to be upwardly mobile as a single parent and still take the time to be involved in my son's life. Society should not penalize women for the fact that we are the ones who get pregnant and are left with the care of the child, either at birth or upon divorce, and we're also the ones who get paid less."

Nicole recognized at the time of the divorce that she had two basic priorities: be a good parent, and become upwardly mobile from an economic standpoint. She took stock of her skills and the wages she could earn, and decided to go back to college and later graduate school.

What do you do if you are a woman raising children as a single parent and money is a problem? Do you choose job training or immediate employment?

With welfare under reform in the United States there is a strong trend to emphasize immediate employment over job training for adult welfare recipients. Many experts now claim that job training is not as effective as simply compelling welfare recipients to get a job. The "short cut" is to help recipients prepare a resume, pursue job leads, master a job interview, and keep a job once it is offered. This view has been supported by research done by the Manpower Demonstration Research Corp. in an assessment of welfare reform programs in three cities: Atlanta, Georgia; Grand Rapids, Michigan; and Riverside, California.[12]

Whether or not you receive public assistance in the form of food stamps or other public monies, we do not recommend taking *any* job just because it is available. Because the wage scales in the United States for low-skill jobs are much lower than in other industrialized countries, the money you earn is not sufficient to support a family of even two—one parent and one child.

Jobs, Money, and the Single-Parent Mother

If the minimum wage in the United States were double what it is now, we would recommend considering immediate employment over a long-term strategy that emphasizes further training or education.

But for a longer-term perspective we suggest the following:

1. Pay attention to skills needed to succeed, either for yourself or for your child. It is important to become aware of the global economy and how the working world is changing. The world of work will not stand still, change is a reality. Low-skilled jobs such as picking fruit and vegetables, patrolling as security guards, cleaning motel and hotel rooms, pumping gas, or waitressing in restaurants will be available but will pay less than "living wages" unless minimum-wage scales are increased substantially.

In the United States college graduates with strong liberal arts backgrounds and communication skills continue to enjoy a thriving job market. There is heavy demand in the areas of engineering, the health professions, pharmacy, and accounting, and it continues in education, both from kindergarten through twelfth grade and at the college and university levels.

2. Check your skills and look for the best job that you can get. Also check on wages. A good source of information is provided by the U.S. Department of Labor (Bureau of Labor Statistics, Washington, D.C. 20212), which evaluates trends in employment and lists jobs expected to increase in the future. It offers valuable information about jobs, careers, and changes in demand for jobs.

The following occupations are expected to grow much faster than average through the year 2005:

chefs, cooks, and other kitchen workers
computer scientists and systems analysts
correction officers
dental hygienists
homemaker and home health aides
insulation workers
licensed practical nurses
management analysts and consultants
medical assistants
nuclear medical technologists
occupational therapists
paralegals
physical therapists
preschool workers
registered nurses
respiratory therapists

restaurant and food service managers
teachers' aides

Education and Training

You must encourage your children to take school seriously and achieve to their maximum ability. If you, as a parent, have not completed high school, do so! Even if you have completed advanced education, review your position and consider furthering your education. Of the mothers that we interviewed, some went on to obtain a master's degree and a license in a health field such as speech pathology, while another obtained a doctorate in education. Both now earn very good salaries. The economic value of education (apart from its other values) can be seen through a selective review of requirements for some of the jobs that will be in demand in the future.

Registered nurses care for sick and injured people and help people stay healthy. To obtain a license, all states require all nurses to graduate from an accredited nursing school and pass a national licensing exam.

Physical therapists help people regain function in basic living skills, including mobility after an illness or injury. New medical technologies save more people from serious injury or illness, increasing the demand for physical therapy. All states require a physical therapist to be licensed, which requires completing an accredited program and passing an exam.

Restaurant and food service managers have a range of duties, including hiring and supervising employees, selecting menu items, ordering supplies, and handling budgets. Since their duties go far beyond those of a short-order cook, most people who hold these jobs have a bachelor's degree or an associate degree in restaurant and food service management. Some private schools offer specialized training in these areas.

We point out this information to highlight the importance of education, especially beyond high school. Not all good paying jobs require a four-year bachelor's degree, but most require education beyond the high school level. Community colleges offer valuable training in preparation for work, and their faculty and counselors are aware of the changing world of work.

Career Counseling

Don't be discouraged by uncertainties in the job market. Colleges offer substantial assistance in this area, such as skill identification and career development. Career counselors at colleges help you practice interviewing, develop a resume, and refer you to jobs.

Setting priorities is a big issue for mothers trying to balance their lives. We spoke with some who returned to college or graduate school while also working and raising children. They will tell you this requires extraordinary commitment and resolve, but education and training are proven ways to increase one's earning power.

Child Support

If you are a divorced woman, presumably the paternity of your children is established. If you had a child born outside a marital relationship, establish paternity. Following the establishment of paternity, insist that there be a binding understanding of child support payments, and do what you can to assure that you receive payments.

Prior to genetic testing it was difficult and often embarrassing for a mother to establish the paternity of her children. She was compelled to testify in court about sexual activities with the alleged father and other persons. But all states now require genetic tests when paternity is contested. These involve a laboratory assessment of samples of blood from the mother, the child, and the alleged father. They can be done at the hospital, a birthing facility, or a medical laboratory. They are accurate and upheld in court.

Child Support Orders

Paula G. Roberts, a lawyer who specializes in family issues, says you need to take seven steps to receive child support:

1. Identify the noncustodial parent.
2. Locate the noncustodial parent. Having the address of the noncustodial parent is important for serving notice of legal action involving child support payments, but also because states only have jurisdiction over persons who live, work, or own property in their state. This complicates child support enforcement when the noncustodial parent moves to another state or country.
3. Serve the noncustodial parent with legal papers. The address of the noncustodial parent must be provided so that a sheriff or other authorized person can deliver legal papers about child support proceedings.
4. Schedule a hearing. We are now at what would seem like step number one. The noncustodial parent must be informed of a court hearing to determine his or her obligations during the child's developmental years—from birth through age eighteen. Scheduling can result in delays because of crowded court dockets.
5. Undertake discovery. The amount of money awarded to you as the custodial parent is based on the financial circumstances of both parents. Information about your assets and those of your child's other parent must be obtained. It is also important to consider the availability of health insurance. Most children of divorced parents in the United States do not have health insurance. Insist that this is provided for your child. It is in the best interest of both the parents and the child to have health insurance.

6. Appear at the hearing. Both you and the other parent must appear at the hearing. If one of you cannot or does not appear, the judge will reschedule it. If repeated hearings are missed, the judge will enter a default order based on failure to appear.

7. The order determines the amount of money that goes to you as the custodial parent for child care. In most states it will go to a government agency that will deduct government funds awarded to your family. Remaining funds will go to you as the custodial parent.

How Much Money Is Available?

In 1991 about five million women in the United States were single parents with children under the age of eighteen. Of those who received child support, the average amount come to $3,143 per year.[13] Of women who bore a child out of wedlock while still teenager, the average annual child support was only $275 per year. The average income of men who parent a child out of wedlock is one-third that of men who marry and then divorce. Men who parent a child out of wedlock are generally not responsible and do not have the resources to pay child support. Many women who bear a child out of wedlock want no further contact with the father and do not seek child support payments from him. This creates a problem when government assistance programs require that paternity is established and that the father contribute to the support of his child. Only 24 percent of unwed mothers are awarded child support.

As a divorced woman, how much child support can you expect? There are two guidelines for determining support: income shares and percentage of income.[14]

Income Shares Formula

The income shares formula is the system that is used in most states. With this system the income of both parents is combined, and a child support obligation is determined using a percentage of income. The support obligation is 18 to 24 percent of net income for one child, 28 to 37 percent for two children, 35 to 46 percent for three children, and up to 46 percent or 61 percent for six or more children. Health care costs are added in and prorated between the parents according to their respective incomes.

Percentage of Income Formula

This system is used by about one-third of the states in the U.S. Awards given to the noncustodial parent are based on a percentage of his or her gross earnings. The award amount for one child is 17 percent of the noncustodial parent's gross income, 25 percent for two children, 29 percent for three children, 31 percent for four children, and 34 percent for five or more children.

Health Care

The issue of health insurance is central to the health and welfare of America's children. Unlike European countries, the United States never instituted a universal health coverage system. Children of divorced or unwed parents are the most likely to be without health insurance, and there are serious problems in implementing health care arrangements. Under our current system a noncustodial parent may be expected to list his or her child under a medical care provision with an employer, which can add several thousands of dollars per year to the cost of hiring an employee.[15]

We urge you to negotiate health insurance coverage for your children as part of a divorce settlement.

Costs of Higher Education

We believe that every divorce settlement should include provisions to cover the cost of a college or university education for the children, but no state requires this. The rationale for excluding funding for higher education costs in divorce settlements seems to be that some two-parent families do not provide funds to cover college expenses for their children, so no divorced parent should be required to pay for college expenses for their youngsters. This is extremely shortsighted, and if your expectations for your children include college or university education, include a financial stipulation in your divorce decree that includes that provision.

What Should You Do If You're Not Getting Child Support?

According to Richard Todd, an attorney who wrote "Collect Your Child Support,"[16] there are steps you can take to collect child support, but it is critical that you have a court order that specifies the amount. If you are not receiving financial support, contact a lawyer and provide the attorney with a copy of your support order and records of monies received and monies due. Give the attorney the address of your former spouse and the information that you have on all assets, including cars, houses, and other possessions.

The attorney can review options and proceed to help you collect child support payments that are due. If your former spouse is employed by a company, the child support payments can be deducted as part of automatic wage withholdings. If your former spouse is self-employed then automatic wage withholdings are not an option. It is then necessary to take legal action against holdings or assets owned by your former spouse.

A Working Single Mother's Point of View

The role of women has changed radically in our century. Historically, women raised children, managed the household, and cared for ill or disabled parents or relatives. Now they continue doing all those things, but they also work. As recently as 1960, women made up one-third of the labor force in the United States. Currently, women make up just a shade less than one-half of our labor force, and even mothers with young children are often employed outside the home. In 1990, 58 percent of mothers with children under six years of age worked outside the home, while in 1965 only 25 percent of mothers with young children were employed. Current changes in welfare require recipient mothers to go to work. While the requirement for work or additional education presents an understandable challenge and burden for women, there is an additional advantage besides independence from welfare: A working single parent presents a good role model for her children if she is successful as a parent. We have seen high school graduates who have stated on their college application forms that they were inspired to pursue their own education by the example set by mothers who managed to continue getting an education while holding down a job and raising a family.

Work Overload

Mothers raising children without a partner still must earn a living and invariably they face work overload. Their tasks include managing family finances, caring for the house and its maintenance, and arranging for child care when they are not available. Then, of course, they are mothers responsible for the day-to-day parenting required to meet the needs of their children.

There are no known ways to reduce the human contact time in raising children. Apart from seeing that their children are well fed with nutritious meals and have adequate clothing, mothers must monitor their children's health and provide medical care, including immunizations and well-baby checkups. They need to enroll their children in school, encourage them, and check on their progress. They also need to find substantial and ongoing time for the "softer stuff" of parenting, from listening and reading to their children to making sure they have opportunities to play with others.

A child should have the chance to develop his talents and interests in sports, music, and other art forms. Also, ongoing contact with extended family and other friends enriches the child's life. Children need discipline and an opportunity to develop values. All of these "little things" take time and energy, and anyone doing them alone is bound to be overwhelmed.

Unreconciled Conflicts With a Former Spouse

Unreconciled conflicts are difficult for all involved, but given the importance of resolving relations with a former spouse, there are two things you will want to remember:

1. While you divorced your husband, your son did not divorce his father. Or, if you are a single father, while you divorced your wife, you did not divorce your child. For your child's sake you will want to keep things as amicable as possible. You will also want to acknowledge the fact that he still has feelings for his father's or mother's parents, aunts, uncles, and cousins. Validate his love for these family members— support efforts for him to still see them, care about them, and have them in his life.

2. There are techniques to make dealing with your son's father easier:
   • Tell him he will always be your son's father and you want to get along for your child's sake.
   • Make your expectations and needs clear.
   • Tell your son's father: "Johnny needs to know we both want him to become a responsible adult and we both care about the rules even if our rules are a little different. What are your rules on homework? My rules are that no TV is watched until homework is done, and I always check it to

make sure it's complete. Johnny's definition of 'done' isn't the same as yours or mine. Can we agree that you will also check his homework when he is with you?"

- Make sure your son's father knows how you feel and why you feel that way.
- Find out how he views topics of concern to him and why. Restate your understanding of his points to let him know you were listening. If you agree, say so. If you disagree, first restate what he is telling you. This may make compromise or agreement possible without a direct confrontation. For example, if he disagrees with your perspective on supervising and checking homework, the following may be a way of restating what he is telling you: "What I hear you saying is that you don't make him do homework because you don't want to spend your time with him doing something that isn't fun." Sometimes the other person will rethink his position when he or she hears how it comes across to someone else.
- Learn the fine art of compromise. "He won't have time to finish his homework on Sunday night when he gets home. You can pick him up on Friday night instead of Saturday if you'll either bring him back early to do his homework here, or do it with him and bring him back at the regular time. But the homework has to be done."
- Keep things cool. Don't accuse or badger. Restate a rationale that brings a focus to the interests of all concerned: "I feel I need support from you on this homework thing. You know how he idealizes you; if you tell him it's important to do his homework and do a good job, he'll do it."
- See a counselor with your ex if communication breaks down.

What Should You Do If You Are a Woman Raising Children as a Single Parent and Money Is Not a Problem

Not every woman who is a single parent is under financial strain. Some have high incomes and manage the transition to single parenting without financial hardship. If this is your situation, you have managed a difficult passage very well. What we suggest is that you pay attention to the national and international scene and consider political action on behalf of issues benefiting families and children.

For example, the United States leads all other Western industrialized countries in the gap between the most wealthy 10 percent of the population and the poorest 10 percent, and many poor persons in the United States do not have regular access to health care. Basic programs for women and children, such as school lunch programs or prenatal health care are being trimmed back. And in many states financial assistance for students attending colleges is also being cut. While individual responsibility is an essential part of being an effective parent, it is helpful to consider what a society can and should do to help support our families. Your perspective, insights—and votes—on these issues can help. We suggest the following:

1. Single parents of young children should not be required to work full-time. Part-time work with full health benefits and flexibility for child care needs should become standard for the benefit of families in our society.
2. Families need access to health care and not just during medical emergencies.
3. Parents who defer career goals because of child care should have access to retraining opportunities.
4. The minimum wage in the United States should be raised to about double what it is now. In Europe wages are set by collective bargaining and are then legally enforced. In the United States we do not have a widespread practice of

collective bargaining, so the federal government sets a minimum wage. Congress should review our fading minimum wage structure and act.

Issues Often Facing Sons Raised Without a Father

Both boys and girls who experience the divorce of their parents face issues and problems that deal directly with the divorce. In addition, sons raised without a father in the home lack the role model a father provides on a day-to-day basis. Sons watch their fathers interact with their mother, the rest of their family, and their community. They learn to handle conflicts, disappointments, and setbacks by participating and observing. When one player (the father) is gone, the son has a hard time understanding a man's perspective. Children confronted with divorce must do the following:

- understand the divorce
- grieve the loss of one parent in the family
- go on with their lives

Grieving the Loss of One Parent in the Home

Children will grieve after a divorce. Their feelings show this sadness in a number of ways. They may be sad or cry and lose interest in activities and people that were important to them. They may have difficulty sleeping because they wonder and worry about what happened and will happen in the future. Their appetite may also change.

There is no set time for grieving, but it will not be over in a week. Grieving normally waxes and wanes, and this is true for adults as well. It is not a steady and consistent down mood, but a cluster of things that come and go and come again.

Grieving is not a disorder. The best "medicine" occurs when

both parents understand and demonstrate caring. Following a divorce a child may have a good visit with the noncustodial parent but be emotionally upset and display it, because the visit may well rekindle what he lost through the divorce. It is helpful if the noncustodial parent who plans to stay involved makes frequent phone calls, sends cards if away, and keeps in touch.

There are many ways for noncustodial fathers to keep in touch:

1. Find out the dates of important events in your son's life. These may include birthdays, holidays, or the end of the school year. Send cards or gifts to let your son know you're thinking of him and are proud of him. Don't wait for him to phone you, follow up with your call.

2. Phone him when you know something is going on in his life, good or bad. One father called his son when he knew he had playoffs coming up. He understood how important the junior high basketball team was to his son, and although he lived in another state he phoned to give his son a pep talk and wish him well. These are little things that mean a lot to a son without his dad being there—it says, "I'm thinking of you."

3. Call your son around the time he arrives home from school—just to say "hello."

4. Take the time to attend special events at school or church in which your son may be involved. Sometimes just showing up tells your son you care.

Going on With Their Lives

Children are resilient, but we should not press their luck. Youngsters will feel and believe their world has fallen apart when their parents say they are getting divorced. The process of going on with their lives involves all the things that belong to normal childhood and growing up: playing, making friends, developing interests and skills in sports, music, art, and feeling connected to family and friends. It also means succeeding in school to the best of one's ability and feeling secure and valued as a human being.

Children of divorce need continued guidance and support from their parents, schools, and the community in dealing with the following problems:

- increased susceptibility to peer pressure
- less success in school
- more likelihood of being sexually active earlier than children raised in two-parent families
- more problems with aggression and the law
- more problems with drugs and alcohol

Children can survive divorce and do well if both parents work together and make the child's needs a high priority.

II

◆ ◆ ◆ ◆ ◆

Fatherless Parenting

3

Positive Parenting

While many single-parent families live bleak lives, it doesn't have to be that way. In the troubled modern world all parents, including happily married couples, face problems brought on by societal changes. It is not the gender of the parent raising the child that creates the problems, but economic conditions, social situations, and emotional stresses.[1] While there is no question that the problems are there, the situation is not hopeless. Mothers can and should start working toward the goal of a better life for their sons and themselves. But how can a single mother, with limited time and money, parent in a way that will reduce some of the risks we reviewed in Part 1? What can you do to improve the situation for your son and yourself?

While there isn't one big, easy solution, there are a lot of little things you can do along the way, day-by-day, that will improve the future for you and your son. Start tomorrow at breakfast or dinner.

Meals Together

Sharing meals improves family life for both children and parents. Pick a time when you can sit down with your child and talk for a few minutes. Breakfast and dinner offer this opportunity for

43

most parents, but your schedule will determine which of those meals works best for you. You will have to organize and plan ahead so that you will have time to talk to your son, but it is worth the effort. You'll want to use the mealtime as an opportunity to talk calmly about what he has planned for the day, any fears or concerns he has for the day ahead, and any events he may be looking forward to. Sometimes children are reluctant to open up, but if a mother begins a conversation with something like this mother used, the child will usually follow the cue:

"Good morning, David. Breakfast will be ready in a few seconds. I'm finishing up the scrambled eggs right now. What's on your schedule for today?"

David just groans, but the frown tells Mom he's worried about something. Mom places a plate of eggs and toast in front of him. "I'm sorry it took a little longer this morning, but I was slow. I keep thinking about what I have to do at work today. Sally, Mr. Nelson's secretary, is out sick, and I have to take her place. If I do a good job maybe I can get her job when she moves to the office downtown, but I keep hoping I won't get nervous and make a big mistake. That's a scary feeling. Did you ever feel like that?"

"On my spelling test, maybe."

"Do you have a test today?"

"No."

Mom's back to square one, so she asks some more questions. "What do you have today?"

"Well, there's math homework due and we have to write something about one of the presidents for class next week, and there's tryouts for the soccer team after school."

"Sounds like a busy day. Which part are you looking forward to most?"

"Coming home. Most of the guys trying out for soccer are better than I am."

"Well, if you practice, you can always get better, and teams need all kinds of players for different positions. I'll

bet you've got a pretty good chance. Why don't you call me
at work when you get home and let me know how your day
went. If you make the team we'll go to McDonald's to
celebrate, and if you don't we'll go out and reward each
other for surviving a rough day. Is it a date?"

"Sure, I'll call you when I get home and let you know."

While this mother chose to use breakfast as her time with her
son, some mothers find dinner works better. At dinnertime even
the preparation can be a parent-child sharing opportunity as
your son helps with peeling carrots or potatoes or other chores.
You'll want to share some part of your day with him and ask how
his went. It is the sharing of feeling, fears, events, and concerns
that inspires children to open up.

One mother always used an old trick her mother used to use
on her. She would tell her son about her experience as a child:
"When I was your age there was a bully at school who used to
pick on me. He scared the life out of me and I had to run home."

She always had a story about her childhood, her fears, and her
survival that related to her son's problems. Sometimes this gives
the child the feeling you've been in his shoes and know how he
feels, and it makes him more willing to tell you his thoughts and
concerns.

Whether you choose breakfast or dinner, plan ahead and spend
at least one meal with your child each day. Use that time as a
special one to keep in touch with your child's thoughts and
feelings.

Work and Play

Chores

Even doing chores together can bring mothers and their sons
closer. For mothers who never have enough time, sharing chores
also reduces their workload while providing time spent in an
activity that offers opportunity for praise and genuine gratitude

for the child's efforts. Some mothers may think, "I could do it twice as fast alone, and my son never does it the right way. I always have to do it over." Patience is a key factor here. Yes, it takes longer to teach him how to fold laundry or mop the floor or clean the tub and wipe down the tiles, but your son will do it correctly and the effort pays off.

When children start to do chores it is important that an adult work with them in the beginning. You would be amazed at the help even a three-year-old can give. Make sure the child sees the activity as fun, not drudgery. Start by doing the chore with your youngster and make it something you both enjoy. Folding warm, fluffy towels fresh from the dryer can be fun when you sit and tell stories while you are folding.

Preschoolers (Three- to Five-Year-Olds)

At this age children can help you fold flat laundry items, like washcloths and towels. They can put their own dirty clothes in a basket and pick up their toys and put them in their proper place (see the following section on structuring the environment). Five-year-olds can help set the table and bring their own dirty dishes to the sink after meals. They can also help with meal preparation and (with supervision) clean their own room and make their own bed (see structuring the environment).

School-Age Children (Six- to Eleven-Year-Olds)

Children in this age group can care for their pet (feeding, walking, and so forth), take clean dishes out of the dishwasher and put them away, and the younger ones (six to eight) usually love washing dishes. Nine- to eleven-year-olds can do some yard work, like raking leaves, pulling weeds, or watering the garden. They can also clean up behind themselves in the bathroom by washing out the sink, toilet, and tub, as well as empty the trash. (All boys should be taught to clean up after themselves.)

It is wise for single mothers to have their sons do their own bathroom chores if they do not have to share a bathroom. If you share the bathroom with your son, take turns doing cleanup, with each one responsible for as much of their own cleanup as possible.

Older children in this age group can also help with meal selection and preparation (especially if you teach them how to work the microwave). Make up a first-aid kit with them, including Band-Aids, burn jell sheets (like 2nd Skin), sterile bandages, scissors, and tweezers. Teach them how to use such a kit. Make sure they have a list of phone numbers they can call for help: your number at the office, grandparents' numbers, neighbors' numbers, and 911.

Junior High (Twelve- to Fourteen-Year-Olds)

Junior high children can do almost anything. They can be taught to iron their own shirts, especially if they insist on buying all-cotton ones. If you teach them how to run the washer and dryer, they can do their own laundry as well. They can also plan, prepare, and serve simple meals. Teach them basic kitchen safety techniques, like how to turn the oven off and on, to always use oven mitts or pot holders to remove dishes from a hot oven, and what to do if they do get a burn (run it under cold water).

They can also baby-sit for their brothers or sisters for an hour or two. At this point they can clean their own rooms thoroughly and even vacuum the house.

By the time your child reaches this age group, in all likelihood he will be home alone after school. Every working mom worries about the danger time—between the hours of 3:00 and 6:00 P.M.—when your son is by himself but you're not home from work. Many mothers try to fill that time with chores or having their sons do homework. While these tasks are fine, there are other options you'll want to consider as well, especially as your child enters the teen years and becomes more socially active and less willing to stay home.

Check after-school activities offered by his school or the community. Explore and discuss these opportunities with your son as you look for a program that matches his interests. You may want to check out classes, clubs, sports, and even work opportunities. Some ambitious children love nothing better than working for two hours after school if a neighbor is willing to pay them five dollars for raking leaves or other yard work. One eleven-year-old, a future veterinarian, makes a thousand dollars a year walking dogs and caring for pets after school. It's something he loves to do and it keeps him busy.

High School (Fifteen-Year-Olds and Up)

High school students think of themselves as grown-ups. At this point you should let them prove it. Remember, if you can do a chore, they can do it. They may require bigger and better rewards, like the use of the car for a special date or a ticket to a concert, but these kids can scrub floors, clean any room thoroughly, and do almost any kind of yard work (mowing, raking, shoveling, and so forth). One mother continued to do all of these things herself until her neighbor told her that she really liked the flyers her son had sent out requesting yard work. "I didn't know he liked yard work so much. I hardly ever see him outside when you're working." When Mom asked him why he never did any yard work at home he commented, "I thought you liked it so much, you'd miss it if I did it for you."

Of course, your son should receive verbal praise for all he has done, and maybe an allowance. You'll want to make sure he knows how much you appreciate his help and reward him, and the time he saves you can be spent doing a fun activity together.

Play

Boys play differently than girls. Gender differences in play are probably more distinctive in childhood than at any other time, even adulthood. It is to the advantage of mothers who raise boys to understand the importance of boys' play, just as it is for fathers to understand girls at play.

We don't want to imply a complete distinction between boys' play and girls' play because there is a spectrum of difference in the play of each. However, it's a mistake to assume that the social development of boys and girls that comes about through play is exactly the same.

Boys at Play

First of all play is a necessary and important part of childhood. A boy cannot grow up and function as a healthy adult without play. When children play they are working on their development. The following observations are for you to think about as you watch your child play:

- Boys often develop friendships around activities, and extensions of their interests and activities may continue throughout life.
- Boys usually develop several major core interests and activities, rarely just one, as they go through their developmental periods.
- Some play interests may fade quickly for children, while others persist throughout their life spans.
- From late preschool years through early adolescence, play is predominantly same-gender play, that is, boys play with boys and girls play with girls.

Competitive Sports

Beyond playing with trucks, cars, and blocks is a more instructive type of play that your son will experience as he grows up, and it includes social lessons and skills used throughout life. Competitive sports, outdoor sports, and even Dungeons and Dragons offer your son opportunities to play with other boys. If you arrange it, your son—at some expense—can enjoy and participate in such sports as tennis, golf, and skiing. Our focus is not to list all of these major play activities, and we're not suggesting these are solely male activities. Also, we know you are familiar with these games and sports, so we won't attempt to explain them. Our intent is to discuss *why* they are important.

Participation in competitive sports can be important because:

- They offer a level playing field, and there may be no other time in your child's life when core skills and attributes can override all other influences. Your child may walk to a playing field or you may drive him there. Another boy may arrive in his parents' BMW or Mercedes or even be chauffeur-driven. It does not matter. Once on the field the game is the only thing that is important, and this is almost universally understood by boys.
- Whatever skills and interests your son develops in sports can be used anywhere; they are transferable. Should you move to another neighborhood, your son's sports interests and skills will help him establish connections with other boys with the same interests.
- Participating in sports will help your child appreciate the level of skill and competition shown by world-class athletes, even though your child may never compete at that level.
- Team play presents an environment in which fair play is valued.

Saying Yes and Saying No

As a single parent, you may feel as though you are always saying no. How can you be more positive when your son asks you to go out and play before he finishes his chores or homework? While this is a problem for all parents, perhaps single moms feel the pressure and pain the most. Saying "no" is hard, but you don't have to use the word no. Let's look at how Sara handled the situation with Mike, her twelve-year-old:

"Mom, I'm going to meet the guys for some ball. I'll be back about eight."
"Oh, Mike. Is your homework done?"
"Almost."
"Let me see it. You know I like to check it over."
"Mom, I'm not a baby and I told the guys I'd meet them. I'm going to be late."
"I have to see the homework first."
"But I've got to go."
"You can go. Just as soon as you finish your homework."
"But I'm going to be late."
"You may go just as soon as you finish your homework."

As you can see, Sara never said "no," even though she was being pressured by Mike. She set limits and told Mike he could go but there was a condition—he had to finish his homework. This method works very well, for it is part of a technique of wording things in the positive and using conditions: "Yes, you may go. Just as soon as you finish your homework."

If your son wants an expensive toy—a Nintendo or the latest, hottest game—try using a condition. "You can have a Nintendo just as soon as you bring your grade in math up to a B." Using this technique sounds so much more positive than saying, "No, you can't have a Nintendo because your grades are too low and I know that if you have that game to play with you'll never do your homework." In the first example Sara gave Mike a goal to work for and held out hope for the Nintendo. In the second example, Mom was critical, negative, and did not offer hope.

Structuring the Environment

One of the ways to get children to help with chores is by structuring their environment. Structuring is really organizing, putting things in order so we can predict where they can be found and what will happen with them. By taking the time to structure you are using a little time now to save a lot later. We all know what it is like to spend an hour looking for something we didn't put away and have forgotten where it is. Somehow, where we put it didn't seem important once, but when we need it— then the hunt is on. So how do we structure our child's environment so that he can do his chores more easily? By using the following techniques:

- breaking down tasks into their fewest basic steps
- adapting standards
- setting priorities
- structuring or organizing the environment
- giving your child rewards and consequences
- being very specific

Breaking Down Tasks

Everything we do is done in a series of steps. Any job can be broken down into smaller steps that a preschooler can do. For example:

- Making a bed is made easier when you eliminate the top sheet and use a comforter that your young son can just pull up every morning.
- Doing dishes should begin with everyone bringing his or her plate to the sink and scraping and rinsing it to be placed in the dishwasher (four- and five-year-olds can do this). When everyone follows, the task of doing dishes is easier because you have eliminated unnecessary steps.
- Putting away toys is made easier by using bins or cardboard boxes for toys with lots of little parts, like blocks or Legos.
- Children will find it easy to dress themselves if laundry is put away on shelves they can easily reach or hung on hooks

at their height. Hooks at a child's height also help him clean his room more easily because he can hang up pajamas and play clothes without difficulty.

- A laundry basket left in the child's closet will teach him to put dirty clothes where they belong.

Adapt Your Standards

You're going to have to adapt your standards to your child's age and capabilities. Six-year-olds cannot clean a room as well as a twelve-year-old, and a twelve-year-old cannot clean it as well as you can. Your standards cannot be met by a six-year-old, and probably not by a twelve-year-old—yet. As your son ages you can expect a little more each and every year, but if you set standards that are impossible for him to meet when he is little he will give up and stop trying.

Set Priorities

Make a list of all the things you think your son can do and that need to be done. Let's say he's an eight-year-old. His everyday tasks can include:

- studying and doing homework
- making his bed
- cleaning the shower after nightly use
- feeding and walking the dog
- packing his backpack for school the next day
- making his own after-school snack
- putting away clean dishes from the dishwasher
- taking out trash

Weekly tasks can include:
- putting away laundry on shelves
- vacuuming and dusting

- helping with meals
- cleaning his bedroom
- cleaning the house

Decide with your son which tasks take priority. What are the most important things for him to get done every day? If doing homework and taking a bath are the most important, then they should be done first, other things can wait. Be sure your child has a say in this too, because he is more likely to get things done if he has had a voice in making the decision.

Remember some of the weekly tasks you will want to do with your son. All children have tasks they really do not like to do. Have your son tell you which ones he really hates and take turns performing those with him. Explain to him that there are tasks that you really hate as well, but they still have to be done.

Organizing the Environment

If you have decided that getting homework done is a priority, you will want to make sure your child has a place to do it. It is always best to set up a spot with your child. Find a place that is comfortable and has all of the necessary elements close by. A desk or table may be ideal, but remember that some children feel most comfortable doing their homework on the floor, which is why it is important to have your child help plan the place.

Also schedule a time to do homework. You may want to keep your son busy until you get home from work. If he is the type of child who doesn't need much help with homework, it may be good to have him do as much as possible beforehand. If he needs help with take-home schoolwork, set a later time and have him do household chores (feeding the dog, vacuuming, or making his bed) until you get home.

Setting Up the Room

All children spend a lot of time in their rooms, and cleaning a bedroom can be made quicker and easier by organizing it. Place similar toys and toys with lots of parts (blocks and Legos) in plastic bins or cardboard boxes. While bins are nice, boxes work just as well and can be dressed up with contact paper for half the price. Pictures of the items they will contain drawn on the front of the box are a great way to help younger children put away their toys. Labels stuck to the edge of a shelf are also helpful. Remember to have shelves and racks at your childrens' level—they'll be more likely to put things on shelves if they are easily reached.

Time Management

Time can inch by when a child is alone and a little frightened. Hopefully, your child isn't home alone until he is at least eleven or twelve. For any child home alone there are lots of things you can do to help him pass the time:

- Make lists of chores for him to do.
- Leave him notes.
- Call around the time he gets home from school.
- Have a trusted neighbor check in on him.
- Arrange for him to visit a friend after school.
- Sign him up for after-school activities, like scouts.
- Have him take a special after-school class like the mentoring program, or homework helpers, in which volunteers come in and help your child after school.

Giving Your Child Rewards and Consequences

All children need to know their work is of value and appreciated. You will want to reward your child with praise and thanks and little things like stickers or pennies. But what children really love is time spent with parents. Rewards in the form of activities are truly rewards for the child and the parent. (More on this in the chapter on discipline.)

Unfortunately, sometimes children need consequences. If your child does something wrong or does not do something he needs to do there may need to be a consequence. Losing a privilege or TV time may be an appropriate consequence. We discuss this topic at length in the chapter on discipline.

Being Very Specific

You will want to make your needs and expectations very clear to your child. Have your son restate what he thinks you said to make sure he understands what is expected. "Homework is to be done before baseball practice" can become "I can do my homework at baseball."

Structuring Your Time

Sometimes it is difficult for mothers to structure time for their children because they have not structured it for themselves. As a single mother it is critical that you structure your time and be as organized as possible. We have listed some tried and true organizational suggestions.

1. Do as much as possible the night before. Make lunches and put them in the refrigerator. Have your son choose his clothes, pack his backpack, and find his shoes.
2. Make your youngster responsible for his property, putting it away and finding it, and for school things—lunch boxes, permission slips, and projects. Have special places for him to put these items when he comes home from school— lunch boxes on the counter, school notes, notices, or permission slips in a basket or shoe box, on Mom's desk, or by the phone.
3. Do things right away. If at all possible, pay bills when they first come in, read mail and dispose of unwanted mail immediately. This way you only have to handle it once.

4. Schedule your time. Do chores on a regular basis: laundry and weekly bills on Mondays, grocery shopping and scrubbing the floors on Tuesdays, and so forth. If you do a little each day you won't have an overwhelming job on the weekend.

5. Learn to do two things at once. Have your son take his homework with him when you must go to the doctor or dentist and help him while you are waiting. Listen to books on tape while driving, or to your son say his part in the school play, his speech, or his spelling words while you drive.

6. Learn to schedule two things together. If you have to take your son for a haircut, find a barbershop near the supermarket so you can run in and get groceries while he has his hair cut. Make sure he understands that he is to wait for you in the shop if he finishes early.

7. Always have something to do when you have to wait. Have a "work bag" with things you can do when you have to wait somewhere—at office appointments, kids' sports games, or other places.

8. Keep calendars and notebooks handy to write down appointments and organize your day when your son can tell you his schedule needs, too. This avoids schedule conflicts.

9. Keep a sense of humor and perspective—there are not enough hours in a day. Remember what is most important in your life—you and your son. Make the most of what you have and always take time to show your son how much you love him.

Teaching Values

Every mother raising a son worries about keeping her son out of gangs, away from drugs, and in school. One of the ways successful mothers do this is by teaching their sons values. While we cover this topic in greater depth in later chapters, values, and how you teach them, are well worth mentioning now. Anyone who has been in a room with a teenage boy for ten minutes knows that lecturing does not work. What does work are a number of smaller, more subtle techniques, like talking about feelings and modeling behaviors you want to see in your son.

Talking, Not Attacking

Sit down and talk to your son about rules and values. By age five children are ready to share in the conversation and understand basic values like cooperation, waiting for turns, and playing fair. It is also important to talk about feelings such as anger, sadness, and disappointment, even with young children. As boys grow older you'll want to talk about values like respect for property and people. Open discussions about feelings and actions when he is angry or unhappy are good techniques for teaching values as well. This is how Ellie handled a situation with Chris, her ten-year-old:

One afternoon when Ellie arrived home she found Chris had punched a hole in his bedroom door.
"Chris, what happened to your door?"
"Someone stole my backpack, and I had everything in it."
"So you punched the door?"
"I'd like to punch out the guy who took it, but I don't know who it was. So I punched the door instead."
"Chris, we need to talk. Tell me how you're feeling."
"I'm upset and mad. Someone stole my backpack, and you can't afford to go out and buy me new stuff."
"I understand how you feel. You're angry, but there are better ways to deal with this. Did destroying the door help you find your backpack?"
"Well, no."
"Now we have to buy a backpack and a door."

"Oops."

"Yes, oops is right. You know when you're angry there are other ways of dealing with those feelings. You could go to a teacher and talk to her. Then you could go to lost and found and fill out a lost item form. You could also look around the school. We can't strike out or destroy property when we're angry or upset. It doesn't solve the problem, it just makes it worse. It's best if we talk about how we feel and what we can do about it."

"I guess I can go to lost and found tomorrow. And next time I'm going to put my name all over my backpack in permanent pen."

"Those are both good ideas. I'll call Aunt Kathy tomorrow and ask her if she still has Ned's backpack. He hasn't used it since he graduated from high school, so maybe she'll give it to you."

Boys have to learn that attacking a child who made them angry or unhappy is not constructive. Learning to talk out their feelings is better. This mom helped her son talk through his problem and think of positive ways to handle it.

Modeling Behavior

We do not always realize it, but what we do everyday in our home has a great effect on our son's behavior. Every mother who wants her son to stay away from drugs must start by making the child's home a drug-free, smoke-free zone. This can be hard, especially if you yourself smoke. If you smoke or do drugs, quit now. If you must smoke, do it outside where your son will not be harmed by secondhand smoke. Mothers really feel pressure when one of their friends comes over to visit and wants to smoke. How you handle this kind of situation will teach your child a lot about coping with peer pressure.

It may be easier if you have a sign posted that says, "Thank You for Not Smoking" or "Drug-Free, Smoke-Free Zone." While a sign will discourage many of your friends from even asking to smoke, what should you do about a friend who does? Maureen, a single mother, ran into just such a problem with her new boyfriend, Bob.

Maureen really liked Bob and didn't want to do anything to drive him away. She had a sign that said, "Thank you for not smoking," but Bob must have felt he knew her well enough that it would be all right.

After a date one evening, Maureen brought Bob home for coffee and to talk. Although the sign hung in the living room, Bob reached for his pack of cigarettes from his shirt pocket, saying lightly, "This is for your other friends, right. It's okay for me, huh?"

For a split second Maureen debated. For years she had told her son about the health problems associated with cigarette smoke. She had told him it was wrong and even illegal for someone to even offer him a cigarette while he was a minor. She didn't want to turn Bob away, yet she knew her son was in the next room.

"No, Bob, It's for everyone. I don't want my son exposed to secondhand smoke. You can go out on the balcony if you want. I'll even keep you company out there if you would like, but no one can smoke in the apartment."

By sticking to her position, Maureen did more than model the importance of drug-free, smoke-free living. She taught her son how to handle peer pressure and that she practices what she preaches. It wasn't until days later that she learned her son had been listening to every word of her conversation. Sons are always interested in what their mothers do and say when they bring a male into the home.

Maureen also made the rules of the house very clear. In posting the sign she was sending a nonconfrontational message to all who could read that her's was a no-smoking zone. The way she handled the situation also sent her son a message. Maureen was firm but pleasant. She was not confrontational or harsh. She simply said no—here is another option: You can smoke on the balcony.

Rules of the House

All mothers should make sure their sons know and understand the rules of the house: No Drugs, No Smoking, and No Weapons. In this day and age, when violence is increasing among young men, we must show our sons more positive ways to handle anger and frustration. Not only must we spell out for them that we treat others with respect, we must teach them that it is wrong to use force or intimidation to get what we want. When we teach our sons to talk things through, by talking with them and listening to them we are modeling behaviors and skills that give them the strength to stay out of gangs.

Dating

Be careful whom you bring home. Your son will learn a lot by watching you and how the men you date treat you. If he sees men treating you with respect and talking through their disagreements with you, he will probably do the same. If you date men who abuse you or behave violently, he may follow their example.

Talk to your son before he starts to date. Make sure he knows and understands that he cannot force a girl to have sex or even fast-talk her into sex. That is rape. In today's society, many young men feel it is important to "score" with girls to prove their manhood. Some even feel siring a child is the ultimate proof of manhood. Make sure your son knows that manhood isn't measured in such "quick and easy" ways.

Real men provide ongoing love, commitment, and support for their families. Real men don't expect you or society (through welfare) to pick up the pieces of their broken promises, relationships, or their tab. All privileges have responsibilities, and sex is an adult privilege with very adult responsibilities. Children are a lifetime commitment. Remind him that you have that commitment to him and that for eighteen years he must be committed to any child he fathers as well.

4

Discipline

While discipline may be a problem for all parents in this day and age, there may be added components that make it especially hard on mothers who have to tackle this difficult area on their own. Not only must they discipline alone, without backup, but research indicates that mothers have a less direct style of discipline than fathers.[1]

One single mother wondered if some of the difficulties mothers face in teaching their sons self-control could be caused by the views of others around them—suggesting a self-fulfilling prophecy at work. She shared her insights with us:

It's my opinion, based on my own experiences, that society holds certain views of women as mothers and of what men need as boys. It can lead people to think that women cannot raise sons without fathers, and it becomes a self-fulfilling prophecy. My parents came to visit when my son was five years old. My mother told me the first day, "Don't worry if he doesn't behave well. We, your father and I, know that a woman can't control a boy, so we won't judge you." Over the course of the next two weeks she learned that my "talking" did work and the last day she told me that she was proud of my skills as a mother.

But that assumption was always there. People were

always telling me that, as a woman, I couldn't control a male child. It's an expectation that becomes a reality. Boys get those messages and then act on them. For example, there have been times when I told my son to do something. If a man was present he would say, "Do what your mother says," as though without a male command he wouldn't do as I asked. My son got those messages, but I talked with him about it. We would discuss why so-and-so told him to do what I asked even though he was already going to do it, and what it meant.

Another problem that comes up is that people don't see cooperation as a viable way of raising a child. A lot of people expect control, and worry that boys without fathers will be "out of control." That has happened to me, often. For example, I encourage my son to speak his mind. To me that is part of being able to create mutually agreed upon "rules." Often other adults would interpret that as disrespect. Sometimes it seems to me that anything short of blind obedience was considered disrespect. While my son was encouraged to talk openly, question things, and assert his view, we also talked respectfully to each other and listened. Some would see that as disrespectful. When my son said "But Mom, I think that I'm old enough to go swimming on my own," and then he presented all of his reasons for thinking that, I know people who interpreted that as disrespectful and as an example of how I didn't have control.

I guess the point of all of this is that sexist assumptions about men, women, and parenting create a set of self-fulfilling sterotypes that make it difficutlt for women to raise sons. We should be asking ourselves why we are so worried about sons without fathers as opposed to daughters without mothers, or sons without mothers, or daughters without fathers. Anyway, that's my opinion as a single mother.

Like most mothers, the mother who shared these thoughts preferred to talk with her child. Mothers tend to reason, explain, and point things out with their children. Women approach parenting differently than men: Men talk less. One can easily jump to the conclusion that the "direct male style" means spanking. Let us assure you, it doesn't have to. While there are differences between a father's and mother's response, there are ways to have more effective discipline.

The Spanking Question

As a parent you may be tired of "experts" telling you not to spank your child. After all, spanking has been around for centuries and it works, right? Not really. While spanking may discipline young children for a short time, it won't work for a long period. Eventually the child will become too big to spank, and there is abundant research to indicate that it doesn't work well. Most parents say they spank to teach their children to either do something, like tell the truth, or not to do something, like run out in the street or talk back to adults. But what spanking really teaches is fear, loss of interest, and aggressive behavior.

Fear

Spanking can create enough fear to make it impossible to perform well. For example, it is difficult for anyone to eat well at meal time if he or she is angry and upset. Harsh punishment for not eating vegetables could cause a child to become upset enough to lose his appetite, and in turn be unwilling to try new foods, even those that are healthy.

Loss of Interest

When spanking is seen by the child as harsh punishment, it may make the child lose interest in the activity for which he is being punished. For example, when a child is punished for making a mistake in his multiplication homework, he may lose interest in math. If spanked for missing a note in music or not practicing, a child may give up his instrument or music all together to avoid failure and punishment.

Teaching Aggressive Behavior

Spanking teaches many children that bigger people can hit someone smaller. Another lesson is that physical aggression is all right if you are really angry.

If you spank we hope you will examine why you spank. Most of the time we spank because we want the child to stop a behavior, like hitting his sister, or because we have caught him doing something that makes us, as parents, very unhappy. When you spank you are modeling the very behavior you want the child to stop. You are hitting out in anger, and instead of teaching the child not to hit you are teaching him that bigger people can hit smaller people to make them do something they want. That is the primary lesson the child learns—one of violence and size. You also want to remember that someday this five-year-old son will be fifteen and much bigger than you are. If he has learned the spanking lesson well, he may hit you to make you change your behavior.[2]

Spanking and Its Consequences

When spanking is used as a method of discipline the result is to inflict physical pain and create fear in an attempt to control the child's behavior. While we do not question the need to discipline children and control their behavior, we have very serious concerns about the use of spanking to discipline children. There are three lessons that may not seem obvious to parents, but they are learned by children exposed to physical force as a means of discipline:[3]

1. Those who love you are the most likely to hurt you.
2. Physical force is okay if the purpose is good.
3. Violence is acceptable as a last resort.

The three points listed above are consistent with findings that adults who are physically violent to their spouse or children had themselves been struck as children. Also, children who are spanked as a form of punishment are more likely to strike a parent or show violence toward a brother or sister than children who are raised with nonviolent forms of discipline.[4]

There are other, long-term problems that can develop as a result of physical force. Adults who experienced severe physical punishment as children show higher than expected rates of clinical depression and alcoholism.[5] This may be because they have a hard time expressing disappointment or disagreement without botching up a relationship. Troubled relationships may continue in adulthood because what was experienced as severe discipline is "carried forward" and now they have difficulty handling day-to-day upsets with a spouse, friends, or children. These problems can set the stage for depression.

People may become rigid and unwilling to try new ventures or activities when they have been punished for making "errors." An "inner script" may tell them to expect failure and disapproval. As adults we all experience situations that require more than one attempt at success. However, when the "inner script" tells us to expect failure we become more prone to depression.

Many parents may say, "Hey, we don't beat our kids. We just give them a whack on the behind." While we understand that there is a range of severity in spanking, from a mild hit on the bottom to an assault with a belt or a stick causing welts and worse, we encourage you to use more nonviolent methods.

Better Ways to Discipline

While violent behavior's message is a major reason to avoid spanking, another far more practical one exists: There are techniques that any mother can learn to make discipline easier and more effective, even with the most difficult children. What works best? We use a simple system of rewards and add consequences if necessary, and also work on giving the child a positive self-concept, because this goes a long way toward making your son a successful, self-assured person who will not need gangs or drugs to feel good about himself.

Mothers often tell you that their sons tend to test limits; they push to see what they can get away with. Some girls may do this as well, but as the mother of a child who "tests the limits" you may find that your youngster needs a motivational nudge to keep him on the straight and narrow. A system of rules, rewards, and consequences arrived at cooperatively by parent and child will provide that motivational nudge.

As we review a system of rewards and consequences, our examples will cover some common issues that all parents face. We see that parents make determined efforts to teach the following values to children:

- Respect the rights of other children and their brothers and sisters (waiting for turns, playing fair, and not disrupting the play of others).
- Express anger or disappointment honestly, without violence or aggression and without running away.
- Be responsible within the family for doing homework and household chores.
- Develop talents that keep doors open for future opportunities.

Rewards

One of the first rules is to know what your child sees as a reward. The two of you may define the word differently. If you say to your son, "If you get all A's on your report card, I'll take you to the opera on Saturday night. We can almost guarantee he will not get A's, even if he is a straight-A student. Young boys do not see an evening at the opera as a reward, a Boyz II Men concert, yes, but the opera, no. You may see that as a reward but your son will not.

Rewards should also remain rewards and not be applied to nonrewarding situations. When Stacy told her son Jason he could go on a weekend ski trip with his dad and his dad's girlfriend, it sounded like a good activity-oriented reward. But it quickly turned into disaster when the four-hour car ride brought out Jason's typical nine-year-old's "Are we almost there?" every twenty minutes, and Dad's impatience. In Dad's eagerness to make the girlfriend feel a part of the activities, Jason felt left out and caused trouble between his dad and his friend.

This could have been avoided with more thought and planning. It would have been better for Jason to have spent a short time with his dad and the new girlfriend until Jason knew her better and Dad's relationship with her had evolved into a more serious, committed one. Even then, a weekend might be too long for a child this age. A reward to Jason would have been a weekend alone with his dad, where he had his undivided attention. Jason's reward wasn't very rewarding for him or his dad.

Your reward can be kept simple and inexpensive: a trip to the zoo, a visit to a relative who lives a couple of hours away, or a "gift certificate" of reading to the child every night from his favorite book. They'll work just as well as expensive games or toys. What you must do is give immediate, tangible acknowledgment to your son for his effort or achievement.

Activity-Oriented Rewards

Most single parents are pinched for money and the idea of buying rewards may sound daunting, but they don't have to be expensive. Sometimes the rewards children like most are your time. Rewards that involve physical activity, time spent with the family, or special time spent alone when the child has your undivided attention can be a huge reward. Taking your child to a baseball game at the high school is a great reward and free. Going to the park, the movies, or on a picnic are inexpensive activities that children love.

Consequences

As we said in the beginning of this chapter, mothers discipline differently than fathers. Mothers tend to explain, give second chances, and are less direct, hoping the child will pick up on the social nuances we provide. Frequently boys don't. Let's look at the different ways a mother and a father handled a situation in which six-year-old Toby and his four-year-old sister Rachel are playing outside on their bikes:

Toby discovered that by bumping the front wheel of his sister's bike he can change her direction rapidly. Rachel has already discovered the best response is a loud wail, "Mom, Toby's crashing into me."

At the first sound of trouble Mom comes running out. She sees the front wheel of Toby's two-wheel bike locked with Rachel's front wheel.

"Oh, did you two crash?"

"No, Toby keeps crashing into my bike."

Mom takes Toby by the hand while patting Rachel with the other hand. "Toby didn't mean to crash into you, honey. I'm sure it was an accident. Now tell Rachel you're sorry."

Toby makes the quick, obligatory "Sorry," and Mom goes back into the house only to hear Rachel's wails three minutes later.

"Mom, he's still doing it."

This time Mom takes Toby's hand and looks him in the eye. "Toby, I'm sure you just wanted to discover how changing the position of a wheel makes the bike change directions, but you're scaring Rachel. Now, play nicely."

Two minutes later, Rachel is really wailing. Now Mom is a little more agitated. She's trying to get dinner done, and Toby is being a pest, not just to Rachel, but to her. "Toby, you're scaring Rachel. If you don't stop it, you're not going to get dessert tonight."

On Rachel's fourth wail, Mom goes out and makes Toby come in where she can keep an eye on him.

Many fathers would respond differently. When Rachel raised her first wail, Dad would probably look up to see what's going on but not rush out right away. If Rachel continued to wail, Dad would go out:

"What's going on?"

"Toby keeps crashing into my bike."

"Toby, why did you do that?" When Toby just looks at Dad, then away to the bike wheels, Dad picks up Toby's bike and says, "Stop pestering your sister, Son."

Dad leaves Toby outside, but takes his bike away.

When we look at how both parents handled this situation, you can see that both did something right. Mom helped Toby to see what Rachel's feeling were. All children need to understand how their behavior is seen by others and how it affects them.

Notice what Dad did: He waited, questioned, and based his action on behavior. Action is a key word here. Fathers tend to act immediately, they don't always give second or third chances, like moms often do. Sometimes they wait to step in as well. While Dad's style of waiting for a second can be helpful, you should assess the situation first. Sometimes it is good to wait, sometimes it is a mistake.

It is very important to encourage your son to express his anger or frustration in words instead of physical action, and violence is decreased when children learn to use words to express their feelings of anger, hostility, or frustration.

When you look at this situation, can you guess which parent successfully kept Toby from plowing into Rachel again? Dad, of course. He used a consequence, and it was one that would be immediate and got Toby's attention. A consequence should be a logical result of behavior, not a natural one. There is a difference between a logical consequence and a natural one. The natural consequence of not doing your homework is to fail the course, but adult perspective tells us that failing the course is a very harsh and complex consequence for a child.

A parent needs to use their adult wisdom and find a logical consequence that is more meaningful to the child, such as loss of privileges. If your child sticks his chewed gum in the piano, he does not get gum for a month. If he breaks his sister's toy, he buys her a new one. If he watched TV instead of doing his homework, he does not see TV for a day.

Also, parents need to separate rights from privileges. Children have "rights" to four things: love, food, shelter, and clothing. Designer clothes, phones, car keys, and toys are all privileges and can be taken away as a means of age-appropriate discipline.

Just as with rewards, make sure you know what the child sees as a consequence. And you should inform your son of the consequence ahead of time—before you enact it. Children are much more likely to respond and cooperate if rules are discussed and agreed on in advance. "If you watch TV after school instead of doing homework or chores, you can't see TV on Saturday morning." Mom threatened this because she wants some control over what her eleven-year-old is watching while he's home alone. That's okay, but rules should always be in the best interest of the child, as well as other family members.

Follow Through

Follow through is crucial. If you told your eleven-year-old he couldn't watch TV on Saturday morning if he didn't finish his chores and homework and neither were done, you'd better be prepared to get up with him on Saturday morning and keep him busy and supervised. It's hard, but it's necessary to mean what you say, and say what you mean.

If you tell your child, "Bobby, you know I don't want you to have friends over to the house after school when I'm not home. If you do it again I'm going to ground you," then if Bobby has someone over without permission you need to be prepared to ground Bobby, with supervision, for the promised time. When you do not carry through with a promised consequence, your child may not believe you or follow your wishes, or, for that matter, trust your word.

It is very important to set up rewards and consequences before they are needed and the situation is calm. In the heat of an argument with a child a parent may make promises or threats they cannot, or do not, want to carry out. This, too, will lead to mistrust. Don't make promises or threats you cannot keep.

Of course, you will want to tell your son the reason for your rules ahead of time: "You know, it really worries me when you bring a friend home and I'm not here. As it is, I worry about what would happen to you if you had an accident, but if one of your friends had an accident his mother would really be angry with me because I wasn't here. I'll tell you what. Twice a month I'll hire Mrs. Adams down the street and then you can bring a friend home. However, if you bring someone home when I'm not here, you're going to be grounded every weekend for a month. I think it's that dangerous."

Be Consistent

Another important approach related to following through is consistency. When spanking is your method of discipline children feel fear, but when you follow through on a consequence other than spanking they feel trust and certainty that you will do what you say. So you must follow through on promised rewards or consequences.

Consistent rules should be established before they have to be used, and should be predictable. They should also be the same at the sitter's, at Mom's house, or when the child is with Mom visiting Grandma. If you have a sitter you will want to sit down with the sitter or former spouse and draw up a disciplinary plan. Think about and discuss what behaviors you want to eliminate and which ones you want to encourage. If you would like your child to share with his brother, you had better reward him when he does so and the sitter also needs to reward him if he shares with his brother. Everyone involved should agree on which behaviors should bear a consequence and decide what those consequences will be.

Rewards work best when they are given every time *in the beginning*. After establishing a behavior rewards should be proffered intermittently. An occasional reward for doing homework or being nice to one's brother after months of doing homework or being nice will make the child feel appreciated as well as reinforce the behavior you wanted. The same is true of consequences.

When everyone is consistent—your ex, a sitter, and you—you can be sure your child will not get mixed messages. Discipline is most successful when both parents and the sitter agree on rewards and consequences, and a disciplinary plan works best if everyone agrees and sticks to it. Hopefully, everyone has the same goal—a happy, well-adjusted child. Point out to the other parent that what is most important here is the child's well-being, and that requires cooperation and consistency on the part of everyone involved in his care. Children learn very quickly who's the softy and who's the cop.

Have the Child Take Responsibility

When it is age-appropriate (somewhere between five to eleven years of age), have your child take part in deciding what would be the best consequence for his behavior. Sometimes role reversal is helpful too:

> "Bobby, if you were the mom, and your son broke your vase, what would you do?"
> Your son may surprise you. He may suggest a consequence more severe than you would have ever thought of (after you've ruled out living with Aunt Judy and Uncle Phil).
> "If I were the mom, I would have really liked that stupid vase, wouldn't I?"
> "Yes, you would."
> "How much did it cost?"
> "About as much as that last Lego set I got you for your birthday."
> "I think I'd make my son sell all of his toys and buy me a new one."
> "That won't be necessary, but you can start by cleaning up the mess. To pay for it you can do some extra chores, or you could give me ten dollars from your bank. Which would you rather do?"

Mom put her son in her place. She placed the value of the vase in terms he could understand, and she gave him options on how to pay off his debt. She also had him clean up his mess. This allows the child to take responsibility for his actions.

When we have the child take responsibility for his actions we achieve two important goals:

- We teach him responsibility and allow him to make amends for his action.
- We relieve ourselves of the anger and frustration we sometimes feel handling everything alone.

Watch Your Words

As adults we sometimes forget how others, especially our children, hear and feel our words. Children can be hurt or abused by words that wound as deeply and scare as badly as any weapon we can use. If we throw a rock at a child it will wound his body, and if your hurl angry words or names at a child it will wound his mind and spirit. Let's look at what happened when Dylan came over to play with Tim:

"Here, Dylan, you be the cement truck and I'll be the bulldozer."

Dylan proceeded to spin the drum of the truck and back it up close to Tim's bulldozer. First Tim moved his bulldozer out of the way, but before he could get a shovel of sand Dylan raised the drum and shouted, "Cement dump."

Tim was anxiously scooping up sand and trying to dump it on Dylan's truck or better yet, Dylan. Soon an argument erupted and Mom had to referee: "Tim, when you have a friend over you want him to have a good time playing."

"Dylan dumped cement on my bulldozer."

Dylan replied, "Well, he dumped sand on my mixer and me."

"Now wait a minute, both of you. Tim, the cement was just pretend, but the sand on Dylan wasn't. And Dylan, when we pretend, it's better to do something both people, not just one, think is fun, like building something together where the bulldozer makes a road and the cement truck comes in and paves it."

When you look at how this mom handled the argument, you can see that she pointed out the problem with the behavior, not the child. She didn't call Dylan a "dummy" or say, "Don't be a bad boy." She criticized the action, not the child. She also gave the boys some suggestions for a more positive way to work together. Had the situation disintegrated further, she could have had both boys take a time out or have them play another way.

Keep Things Positive

Just by employing the positive rather than the negative,

parents can change the behavior of a child, because children respond to a positive direction rather than a negative command. If you say, "Please get off the chair and put your feet on the floor," you will make more sense to a child than if you say, "Don't stand on the chair." In the first example the child is given an action to follow, not one to stop.

Also, parents soon discover that what worked on a two-year-old doesn't work with the same child in fourth grade, and what works with a fourth grader won't work when he's in high school.

When we look at what Mom did in the previous situation we can see that she did a number of things very well. She stated her concerns clearly, and she told Tim and Dylan what was expected. Had the boys continued to fight Mom would want to do the following:

- Explain what the reward for cooperation is: Play together twice a week and build bigger and better roads.
- Tell the boys what the consequence is: They must take a time out, and if fighting continues Dylan must go home.

For discipline to be effective it should be age-appropriate, taking into consideration the child's age, abilities, and needs.

Age-Appropriate Discipline

Two- to Four-Year-Olds

At this age young children are equipped to explore and actively engage their environment. Language and beginning-number concepts, such as counting and grouping develop rapidly, but children develop social skills more slowly. As they learn cooperation and sharing, it is helpful to offer them opportunities to play with other children in fun and interesting activities. Young boys and girls in this age bracket have some basic needs:

- being wanted and needed
- being cared for and protected
- being valued, accepted, and given a sense of belonging
- being given opportunities for exploration, play, and the development of self-care skills, such as dressing themselves and toilet training

Normal two-year-olds are busy little guys, as every parent who has ever had one knows. Frequently we will hear mothers say, "He was such a good baby. Now, all he says is 'No,' and 'I do it myself.' He is driving me crazy."

As part of the growing-up process, all two-year-olds try to assert themselves. What all parents should know is that every child needs discipline in every stage of development, especially when they are in danger of hurting themselves or someone else. Let's look at some of the best ways to handle children in different age groups starting with two- to four-year-olds. (You will also want to use some of the techniques we have already talked about.)

- Keep things positive. Use positively-worded directions. Instead of "no," tell the child what he must do.
- Use a system of rewards and consequences. Use rewards first and both rewards and consequences immediately.
- When you are working with little children, *ignore bad behavior if it isn't hurting anyone.*

Handling Problem Behavior

It is hard for all of us to ignore bad behavior, but when it comes to temper tantrums, ignoring them is one of the best ways to eliminate them. When you see a tantrum coming on it is a good idea to tell your two- or three-year-old that it is okay to kick and scream, but that you don't want to see it. Tell him he can yell all he wants to in his bedroom and on the floor, where he is safe. After you, his audience, are gone the tantrum will stop, and when you eliminate the audience, you eliminate the tantrum.

Children learn very quickly: Why bother if no one is watching? After the child calms down it is helpful to have him tell you how he felt. Was he sad or angry? He may tell you he really wanted a toy someone else had. While you may not be able to satisfy his wishes, point out that you will listen to him when he is upset or angry. Having him tell you about what bothered him will teach him a better way to get your attention and make tantrums less productive.

Mothers always tell us, "This method works fine at home, but he always has his tantrums in the store or somewhere equally embarrassing. What should I do then?" We suggest the following:

1. Try to avoid situations that will be difficult, like shopping before nap time or when your child is going to be hungry.
2. Avoid long outings in places of little interest to small children, like the supermarket or department store.
3. If you cannot avoid the situation, come prepared with toys to keep him occupied and a snack.
4. Reward him when he doesn't have a tantrum. In the beginning it is important to reward your son every time you take him shopping and he does not act up. Read him a story when you get home, or take him for a bike ride. Then you will want to reduce the rewards to occasional or intermittent ones. Be sure to tell him why he is being rewarded: "Mike, you were such a good shopper. I'm going to take you to the zoo for being so good."
5. Never ignore bad behavior that will hurt another person or property. Explain that he is not to hurt someone or break things when he is angry.

Five- to Seven-Year-Olds

For single moms these can be wonderful years. Your son is old enough to really sit down and talk with you about how he feels and what he thinks. Keeping in touch with him and how he sees his world is interesting and opens a door for parent-child communication. He is ready to understand reasons for the rules you set. In talking to your child about rules and values he begins to understand the importance of cooperation, playing fair, and waiting one's turn.

As a parent, you may have concerns about the television programs your child is exposed to. Violent programs are carefully designed to be interesting to young children, especially boys. While we cannot ask our sons not to be interested, we can control and guide what they watch on TV. At this age it is helpful to explain to your children that some programs are off limits: Those featuring violence and aggression, including some Saturday morning cartoons, are not considered entertainment in your home. Setting rules for entertainment programing with children between the ages of five and seven makes it possible to maintain an influence on them later on.

Talk to your son about his feelings when you sense sadness, anger, or dissappointment. Ask him to tell you about it. Remind him that if someone makes him angry, it is better not to attack or become aggressive. Boys need guidance to help them express their feelings and to think out civil and positive ways to handle situations. It's interesting to note that teenage boys and adult males with violent behavior usually experienced aggressive behavior between the ages of five and seven, so you can see why it is important to talk to your son while he is still young enough to learn better ways to handle anger and frustration.

At this age your son has a personality, can help you in the house to some degree, and is becoming a real person. Remember that this is a period in his life when family and parents still have a strong influence on his life, so it becomes very important to work on positive discipline and building a positive self-concept now.

Some techniques for five- to seven-year-olds:

- Use a system of rewards and consequences.
- Reward good behavior immediately.
- Provide activity-oriented rewards.
- Call time outs when bad behavior develops.
- Have your son take more responsibility for his actions.
- Give your son a voice in the consequences for bad behavior.

Some things for Mom to work on:

- consistent discipline
- specifically stating rules
- stating rules before trouble begins
- limiting options
- choosing your battles

Eight- to Eleven-Year-Olds

During these years your child establishes a footing to secure himself in adolesence. Your influence is critical and includes guidelines for behavior and a rationale for the values you instill. You also, need to monitor how well he is doing in school and be responsive to his readiness to learn and test himself.

His circle of friends will expand and include more boys than when he was younger. As he develops new interests his activities will include new friends and acquaintances. If scouting or other similar activities are available he may develop friendships while participating in group activities. While working on a project or merit badge, he may show persistence that will surprise you. Also, he is less dependent on immediate results and more willing to wait. Keep in mind that he is developing life skills and a readiness to persist when things are difficult.

He is capable of helping with household chores and may be more willing to help if they are understood to be an important part of family life and not busy work. Boys this age can help with the care of younger children by reading to them or playing with them if you demonstrate some of these skills first. Although they can help with child care, boys this age are not old enough to be responsible when you are not home.

You will want to keep in touch with your son's school, monitor his schoolwork, and ask for a conference if problems develop.

Peer Pressures

Many parents think that peer pressure doesn't begin until high school, but that is not the case. It begins early, with innocent requests like your son asking for the same toys all of his friends at school have, and it will progress to more serious things even at this early age.

Unfortunately, your child will probably be offered a cigarette while he is still in elementary school. The offer will come from a "friend" while you are not present. The friendship, if it is an important one, will not end if your son refuses. Talk to him about this and say that it is wrong for someone to offer you a cigarette and that he should refuse it. Have him tell you about it and be prepared to call his friend's family and explain that you do not want your son to be given tobacco in any form. The same is true for alcohol and drugs.

Establish a rationale for your child. Explain that tobacco, alcohol, and drugs are bad for his health and they are addictive. He may not understand the word *addictive*, but tell him that these can "take over," be harmful, and hard to stop using.

Guns

It is dangerous to have guns and children in the same home. If you have a gun it should be securely locked up at all times. The gun and the ammunition should be stored separately, and the ammunition should be under lock and key. As a single mother, you may feel you need a gun for protection, but for every gun used against a criminal in self-protection about forty relatives or friends are accidently injured or killed, or the gun is used in a suicide or an impulsive act of rage.

If you have a gun, explain to your son that they are used for hunting and always must be locked away. Tell him that if he is at a friend's home and his friend wants to show him a gun, he should tell his friend he needs to go home. Then he should return home and tell you about it.

Twelve- to Eighteen-Year-Olds

You might think that none of the techniques we mentioned will work with teens. Many parents even say, "Nothing works with teens." You can say that, but it just isn't true. While consequences may differ for teenagers, the same system of rewards and consequences will work for them. To successfully manage teens—and your sanity—you will have to use rewards and consequences. Without consequences a parent quickly finds their teenager is running the house as they helplessly stand by. That's what happened with Lamont and his mom.

Lamont

As a child Lamont was difficult; now at fourteen he does not want anyone to tell him what to do. One evening, when his mother had her friend over for dinner, Lamont and his friends were loud and rude. His mother asked him to have his friends come back later. In anger, Lamont stormed out of the house and didn't return all night.

During his early childhood, Lamont's mother loved him very much. She felt bad that his father had deserted them and she hesitated to discipline him because she felt he had been "hurt enough." In an effort to build up his self-esteem she praised him for the least little thing but rarely had consequences for bad behavior. At this point in her life, Lamont's mother is almost afraid of her own son. How can she maintain discipline when her son is so out of control?

Lamont's age is an issue. When a five-year-old boy gets very angry and believes he has been treated unfairly he may pack a bag, sneak out of the house, and go as far as the end of the street before getting tired, hungry, or even lonely, and return home. When a fourteen-year-old leaves the house after an argument, the problem is obviously more serious.

Long-term runaway teenagers believe that they are unacceptable to the family and will be ostracized or endangered by remaining at home. Teenagers who discover that they are homosexual are especially vulnerable because they fear rejection by their families. Children who have been abused are also at risk to run away and face the extreme risk of becoming homeless. It is extremely rare that what occurred between Lamont and his mother would lead to a long-term runaway situation for a teenage boy (or girl). However, in an increasingly dangerous world, having a child gone overnight would frighten any mother.

In Lamont's case, the problem was that he was overprotected. His evening didn't go as he planned and his mother "spoiled it." What should Lamont's mother have done?

When Lamont returned, probably the next day, his mother should have explained that she is glad to see him back in the house, but that she remains upset that he left without her permission. Then she should tell him that she would like to know what disturbed him, but at the end also explain her point of view, and they should arrive at an agreed-upon solution to prevent the problem from happening again. The agreement must leave the mother as *parent*.

Teen Problems

As teens mature, mothers face a number of problems, some old, some new. School, peer pressure, and discipline are still on the list, but there is more. Mom has to worry about dating, drugs, alcohol, and even depression. Discipline for teens includes the need for praise, rules, rewards for good behavior, and consequences for unacceptable behavior. Do not be afraid to take away car keys, curtail activities, or remove privileges, but some of the techniques you used when they were younger will not work with teenagers. Jeff's story is one many mothers experience with their teenage sons.

Jeff

At fifteen, Jeff was bored, frustrated, and growing apathetic. His schoolwork was beyond the "quick-fix" stage, and most subjects were going poorly. Although he was in the ninth grade, his reading and math scores were at the fifth-grade level. Problems that began in the lower grades compounded, creating a widening gap between his performance and his grade level. Most of the time he wouldn't answer questions in his math or literature class because he was afraid the other kids would think he was stupid. He was shy, immature, and insecure. His mother requested a progress review with his teachers, who went over his academic performance and his problems. Jeff showed all of the following:

He appeared tired in class.
He had trouble communicating with students and teachers.
He showed little interest or enthusiasm.

What concerned his teachers the most was his lack of interest and general apathy. Jeff's mother noticed the same kind of behavior at home and felt her son was vulnerable. Adolescence is a time when teens try to separate themselves from their dependence on their parents and strive to find a place to fit into the larger world they are discovering. Jeff's mother realized that teenage boys are vulnerable to bad teen pressure, early sex, alcohol and drug use, and delinquency if they become apathetic, dissatisfied, and are doing poorly in general.

While Jeff was not doing well, he did have interests he had not yet developed. One of his teachers suggested a mentoring program that uses foster grandparents, and his mother made the contact.

The man met with Jeff and helped him with his reading and encouraged him in his schoolwork. As a retired gentleman, he had the time to demonstrate woodworking skills, and he taught Jeff how to do some basic woodwork and building projects. Together they planned and constructed a twelve-foot wooden boat. Jeff learned to read building plans, make measurements, and cut, assemble, and paint all as part of building his boat. He looked forward to working with his "grandfather" and was responsive and interested in everything he was learning from him. Every session reinforced the values his mother had taught at home: loyalty, helping others, developing skills, and experiencing satisfaction from doing something you like and doing it well.

Part of discipline in a family is sensing a child's distress or apathy and coming up with a plan or opportunity for the teen to regain a sense of optimism and purpose. Jeff's "grandfather" accepted him and gave him opportunities to experience satisfaction through work and creativity. His continued help gave Jeff the boost he needed through his teen years.

With teens, negotiation and contracts are helpful. All teenagers like to express their independence, they do not want you to "run" their lives. Sometimes they do not want parents to tell them what time to get in or what they can and cannot do. While teens need to express their views on topics and you should listen to their views, you have to remember that a teenager is not an adult yet; he is not ready to run his own life yet. You must monitor, and you have the final say.

When you reach an impasse with your teenager, a contract may be the best solution. Contracting is a management technique that spells out in writing what your son and you expect from each other. Sit down with your teenager and draw up a contract. Spell out what the rules are, what you expect him to do, what he expects from you, and what the consequences and rewards will be. Remember to negotiate this contract. A simple contract could read like:

Chris Johnson will get paid for chores he does in the house when they are finished. After school he will come directly home and do his homework for a period of two hours. Upon completing his homework he will go to his soccer game. He will notify his mother at work, by phone, where he is if he is anywhere else besides at school, home, or soccer.

His mother, Catharine Johnson, will not enter his room or snoop through his things without permission. Chris can invite friends to the house if he gets permission first. Chris can plan to play soccer anytime he wants if his homework is done.

Be sure to spell out consequences and put everything in writing. You and your son should both sign and date the contract.

Discipline doesn't have to be difficult. It doesn't even have to be negative. But it should be consistent and fair, and parents have to have the self-discipline to discipline their child.

5

Positive School Experiences

As we previously noted, research clearly indicates that children in single-parent families are less likely to finish high school, let alone go on to college. It is commonly believed that children do best with the same-sex parent; boys being raised by mothers alone are at greater risk, but it is not that cut and dry.[1] Other factors come into play: the economic status of the parent, the neighborhood in which the child lives, and whether or not there is extended family and friends to give emotional support. In today's high-tech society each child needs as much education as he can possibly get, and one of the greatest risks sons without fathers face is the lower economic status brought on by dropping out of school.[2]

Single mothers face the same school-related problems as two-parent families. We asked Lorri what problems she faced as a single mom while her son was in school.

One of the things I remember most clearly about Josh's elementary years was that I always felt bad when I couldn't help on class trips or projects. I was working part-time and going to school. I hated "open-house" night at school because I knew that spending two-and-a-half hours at Josh's school meant I would be up until midnight finishing my homework. Josh was great. I'm sure it was hard on him when the class had father and son lunch day and his father didn't show up.

There were rough times for him. Occasionally one of the other kids would make a comment about his father, or lack of one. So many kids come from single-parent homes now, though, that that wasn't too big a problem. But I can still remember the sad look on his face when Tom, our neighbor, was talking about how his father was teaching him to ski on a family ski trip—that was probably the hardest. I know it must have hurt him at times.

Junior high was pretty miserable for both of us. I was trying to get established in my career and Josh was trying to survive. It's hard on all kids that age, but he had to deal with bullies, trying to fit in, and he had to go home to an empty house. He got involved in the soccer program and that saved our lives. He had practice almost every day, and he made some good friends on the team. He got to know Danny, who lives three blocks away, and his dad was the assistant coach.

High school was better in some ways, but worse in others. In high school there are more classes and choices, but it can be scary too. For a while he wasn't very interested in anything and I was petrified he would end up in a gang. Then he took drafting and the drafting teacher encouraged him. Somehow he got interested in architecture and landscape architecture. That's what he's in now in college. That and soccer really helped.

Lorri faced some of the special problems single mothers experience. She was so overloaded with jobs at home and work that she couldn't give her son's school life as much attention as she would have liked. She also felt that her son had more responsibility than most kids his age and she worried about bullies and him being home alone. She also worried about her son dropping out of school when he was losing interest and motivational steam. In Lorri's case her son was helped by a sports program and finding things in which he was interested—drafting and architecture. Many single mothers face the same concerns.

How can mothers encourage their sons to stay in school and go to college or continue on for training? There are a number of things that can be done to improve the odds.

First, adopt the policy that if your child is capable of it, college is a must. Before you say, "I can't afford the rent, how can I pay for college?" you can. There are all kinds of low-cost grants, loans, and full scholarships available for low-income children. High schools have computer scholarship search programs that will tell you about any scholarships for which your son would qualify. You can also access the Internet with key words like *scholarships* and find information on funding. The information we give in our chapter, "Improving Your Financial Picture" will also apply to your son.

The money is there. What has to be there on your part is the desire and ability to deal with this question. You have to convince your son every day of his life that college is not an option. It is a necessity. For generations immigrants who came to this country have known that the way to improve your status and that of your family's is through education. Getting as much as you possibly can is not the fastest or easiest way to improve your life, but it is the surest, and there are many things you can do to make education a goal your son will want to achieve.

Reading Ritual

From the time that he is little read to him, and let him see you reading. If reading is a problem for you or him, get help. There are any number of programs, like Reading Is Fundamental (RIF) that help adults and children learn to read.

Talking about school is one of the little things you can do. Each and every day discuss with your child what's going on in school: What project is he working on? What is he studying? Does he like a particular subject? Does he find it interesting? How would he apply what he is learning to his life? Talk about school as a positive thing that will help him with his life today and in the future. Ask the teacher what she or he is teaching and talk to your son about it. A three-part "earth unit": underground, above the ground, and in the sky inspired this discussion between Jason and his mother:

> They study such interesting things in school now. When I was in second grade we didn't do much science. But you're doing neat stuff, earthworms below the ground, trees and plants, and weather and clouds in the sky. It makes me want to go back to school and become a plant doctor or an astronaut. Next time you dig up an earthworm or pull a carrot out of the garden you'll know a lot more about it, right Jason?

Working with teachers on discipline and other issues that concern your son or his school is another big key. Children need to feel that you and the school are working together. If he is having problems with math, he needs to know that you have talked to his math teacher, and that you're going to check his papers to make sure he isn't having trouble with the problems and did all of them. If he's still having difficulty he should know that there will be someone at home or at school who is willing to help him work on it.

The same goes for behavioral problems. It is important that your son knows you are not ganging up on him, but that you and the school stay in contact and work on his problems and concerns together. Reassure him that you love him, but that there are problems that have to be worked on.

Volunteering in the Classroom and for the PTA

One of the best ways to eliminate behavioral problems in the classroom is parent involvement. Children behave much better when their mom, or someone else's mom, is in the classroom. It's hard to volunteer once a week or once a month when you have a job and have to work to feed the family. But many businesses will give you two hours off once a month to volunteer, and you may be able to arrange to come in to the office two hours later once a month and make up the time by working two hours later that day. You could be surprised if you look into it. If your job is the least bit flexible this could be well worth your time. Volunteering has an added benefit: You get to know the teachers and can learn more about your son's school and his life at school.

Nightly Homework Review and Weekly Notebook Review

It is important to monitor your child's progress in school. Sit down with him and check his notebook. Look at his papers when they come home each day, and make a big deal about papers with A's and B's. You'll be amazed at what you can learn from looking through his notebook with him. Not only will you see how his work is progressing, you'll find notes from the teacher and gather tidbits about what is going on in school. Sometimes you even find his newest girlfriend's name scribbled on the back jacket, but try to ignore that unless you son shows a willingness to talk about it. However, it is vital to check homework with him and make sure he is doing it and producing good quality work. Here, again, it is important to keep in touch with the teachers. Ask if there are any problem areas for your son.

One of the ways you convince your child that school is important is by making sure he knows how important it is to attend everyday. If your child says he doesn't feel good and wants to stay home, make sure he isn't rewarded with a morning of cartoons or other TV programs. If he's sick enough to stay home, he's sick enough to be in bed with "quiet" activities like reading. This may mean disconnecting the TV before you go to work or leaving instructions with the sitter: "No TV." Some cable companies will soon be offering a specially-coded box for parents to "turn off" the TV when they can't be there to supervise their child's viewing of programs. You need to give the child the message that going to school is really important, and that you have to be *really* sick to stay home from school.

A Time and Place

Organizing and structuring time is important, and it is important to set aside a certain time everyday to do homework. Have your child help pick a time when he can do his homework and you can be there to help. Some children like to do their homework as soon as they get home from school so they can get it out of the way while others prefer to take a break, eat dinner, then take out their homework. You will want to do whatever your child feels most comfortable with, but you will want to sit down with your son and pick a time for him to do his homework every night. One mother, a college student herself, sat at the dining room table with her son and they did their homework together. Since he was in high school they could help each other. They both gained enormously from this structured time, and both mother and son found their grades improved.

It is also important to have a place to do homework. Some children are comfortable in beanbag chairs, while others need to sit in a straight-back dining room chair. You and your child will want to decide on a place that provides:

- good light for reading
- enough quiet for study
- closeness to Mom so she can monitor
- a comfortable chair
- needed materials close at hand
- enough room to spread out materials such as notebooks and pens

It doesn't matter if your son does his homework at the dining room table or in a beanbag chair in his room. What matters is that he follows a routine, that he does his work, and that you check it in his earlier years. Unless your child has a learning disability like Attention Deficit Hyperactivity Disorder (ADHD) or another disability, he is probably old enough—and responsible enough— to do his homework. However, if your son is like Sara's Mike—in the habit of sneaking out without doing his chores or homework—you will need to check sporadically.

When the School Is a Problem

Paula was a thirty-eight-year-old divorced mother of two boys, Dwight and Dave. Dwight was an honor student, class officer, and top athlete. Dave was a poor student, had questionable friends, and hated school. Needless to say, Paula heard from Dave's teachers a lot. When she was called into school, often teachers would tell her they felt Dave's problems were due to the divorce, yet she had raised the two boys exactly the same. It wasn't until both were grown that Paula learned that Dave had a learning disability.

We share Paula's story for a very specific reason: Paula had faced an unspoken prejudice. Many schools feel that children from single-parent homes are bound to have difficulties and may blame a child's problems on his home, overlooking the real underlying problem. As a parent you need to be aware that schools may have this attitude, and when you know that your home is not a factor, be sure to talk to the teachers or administrators and encourage them to look more carefully at problem areas.

While we have talked about how important it is to work with the school for your son's sake, we know that things do not always go well with schools. What should you do if that is so?

The first thing you should do is talk with the person your son is having the problem with. If this is the gym teacher, by all means talk with the teacher. If he is experiencing problems with the lunchroom monitor, talk to that teacher. Keep in mind that high school boys may not want you to "interfere." Talk to your son. Ask him if it would help if you spoke with the teacher.

Next, talk with the guidance counselor. He or she can be very helpful when there are problems at school. Some are talented and insightful and can offer ideas on ways to solve the problem and avoid future ones.

If you are still having problems with the school go to the principal.

If your son is having behavioral or academic problems, we encourage you to have the school do a thorough evaluation of your child. Don't stop working on his problems until they are solved and you feel comfortable that your son's situation is improving, because his education is important to his future.

Attitudes Toward School

We give our children messages in everything we say and do, and your attitude toward school is contagious. If you believe that education is very important, your son will believe it too, and he will try harder and work to achieve. However, even if you say education is important but allow him to skip school, criticize his teachers, and you show no interest in learning yourself, he will not value education.

If we want our children to get a good education we must work *with* the schools and *on* them too. One single mother, Celeste, was not very good in math. While her son liked math, every once in a while he would run into a problem with the subject and start to dislike it.

Celeste felt math would be important to her son's education, so she called the school and asked if they had anyone who could tutor her son. The school, in a poor neighborhood, did not have an after-school tutoring program, so Celeste called the school district and asked what it would take to get one started. They told her, "an act of Congress": The district simply did not have the money to do something like that.

Celeste did not give up. Her son needed help in math and she couldn't help him. She kept remembering something she had learned in her math class—every problem has a solution. Celeste called a local college hoping to learn how to go about setting up an after-school tutoring program. She talked to a professor in the education department, and he gave her some ideas, names, and phone numbers. He suggested some fraternities might be willing to take on an after-school tutoring program as a project, or perhaps the education department would be willing to set up a program using students.

After pursuing each lead, Celeste did find a group to take on the project. Her persistance and desire to help her son paid off. She worked both with and on the school and achieved something very special for him and other children.

Having parents in the classroom can also enrich life for all children, and we know that children are better behaved when parents are helping at school. Of course, you will want to ask the teacher if and how you can help, for some have specific jobs they want or need a parent to do.

After reading about the importance of learning a second language early in life, one mother became concerned that her son was missing out because his school did not offer foreign languages until sixth grade. She knew of a neighbor who had grown up in France and spoke fluent French. After talking to the neighbor and the first-grade teacher, the neighbor went to school one day a week and taught French for two hours every Tuesday. The neighbor truly enjoyed sharing her first language with the children, and the children loved learning French.

Both of these mothers made a difference in their child's life and education, and they did it with nothing but love and determination. They had a positive attitude. They worked with the school. And they made a difference.

III

❖ ❖ ❖ ❖ ❖

Areas of Concern

6

Improving Your Financial Picture

After decades of watching families suffer through divorce proceedings, our judicial system decided to overhaul divorce laws. No-fault divorce was originally intended to reduce rancor and blame, but the result leaves many middle- and upper-class women poor. Anyone who works in the social welfare system will tell you that the courts' good intentions never considered the penalty even educated women must pay for putting their careers on hold to help a husband establish himself or nurture their children during their early years. While her husband's career is taking off the stay-at-home mom is watching her children—and her job skills—age. Even wealthy women can be thrown into poverty by a husband who doesn't make his child support payments, and rarely will she know where to turn for help or how to begin to look for it.

Perhaps there is no poorer segment in our society than single women raising children alone. Of the single-parent families headed by women, half are living below the poverty line,[1] and some of these families will end up homeless. If a mother with children ranging in age from toddlers to teens wants to use a homeless shelter, often she must be separated from her teenage son, because teenage boys are sometimes excluded from shelters.[2]

While not every single mother is in poverty, all too often most single mothers face this situation at some time. One mother told us that most of her single friends experienced "creative poverty" even though they lived in nice homes in good neighborhoods. Alise, a single mother with whom we spoke, is an example.

Although she was granted the $250,000 family home and child support, Alise found herself down to her last ten dollars when her husband stopped making his monthly payments. The divorce decree ordered her to split the profit from the house at the time of sale, so she was reluctant to sell it. She was caught in a Catch-22 situation: Sell the house and take the fifty thousand dollars after taxes but pay double the house payments in rent, or stay in the house with low monthly mortgage payments and have the courts pursue child support while she tried to survive on the little money she made working part-time while attending classes.

We know and understand how difficult it is for mothers, already in poverty and overwhelmed with demands on their time and money, to even consider taking on bigger and more frightening tasks like returning to school. Yet it is clearly the best way to escape poverty, though not the quickest nor easiest.

To make matters worse, government aid continues to shrink, and women find they must become more and more self-sufficient. We understand that most women would rather not be on welfare, but the truth is that many women must have some sort of government help to survive for a period of time, however short. New welfare reform laws make training and education not only desirable but necessary.

Under the new welfare reforms, most states will require mothers to enter jobs programs to keep their welfare checks. They will be able to continue to receive welfare as long as they are in a jobs program or in school, but if they drop out they may lose their welfare altogether. More and more states are implementing the two-year rule: No one can stay on welfare for more than two years out of every seven. However, the two-year rule does not apply as long as you are in the jobs training program or in college and continue to make good academic progress.

Forgive us if we push, but we feel we can not state it strongly enough: Get as much education as you can or as much job training as possible. Look into traditionally "male" jobs that may be higher paying as well: plumbing, truck driving, welding, or driving a forklift, to name a few. Many of these jobs do not require brute strength, just skills that can be learned.

In Chapter 2 we talked about the importance of getting as much education as possible. We even gave a list of good-paying jobs that require training or education for four years or less. We would like to encourage you to study the list carefully. After you've done so, call a junior or community college and go over a jobs list with a career counselor who can help you analyze your interests, talents, strengths and goals. If that step seems frightening, start smaller.

Almost every high school and community or junior college has a computer program that will ask you questions and match your answers with jobs. On the West Coast most high schools and community colleges use a program called the Career Information System, or CIS for short. Internet also has a program in use and can be accessed by typing in key words like "career info."

Call the community colleges in your area and ask what type of computer program they use. The programs take the answers you type in and give you a printout of jobs and programs that suit your interests and skills. You may go to any public high school or community college and use them. Most of the community colleges we contacted were happy to offer any help you may need and only asked that you make an appointment so they would have time to help.

After that, make an appointment with a guidance or career counselor. Counselors are usually willing to talk to you, but if they don't have time the jobs program office or a social worker at the county health department could put you in touch with someone to help sort out job training prospects.

Most programs require a high school degree on entry. If you do not have one, don't despair. You can always get a GED (Graduate Equivalency Degree) and in most places community colleges offer GED courses. To get a GED you will want to talk to a counselor at the community college and enroll in the GED courses she or he recommends.

By all means don't rule out community colleges or even universities because you're worried about money or child care. The fact is, most community colleges and universities have day care available, and every financial aid department can tell you ways to finance your education. Every social worker we interviewed said that if someone really *wants* to go to college, and has the *ability* and *desire*, some type of financial package can usually be put together for them. Some single moms actually find that it is to their advantage to attend a community college or university when they consider the grants, loans, and low-cost day care they offer. The long-term payoff is always to your benefit, so give this some careful thought.

Financial Aid

To begin this process, you will want to go to the financial aid department of the junior college or university and make an appointment with one of its counselors. All financial aid departments have a computer program listing scholarships, and the counselor will give you more information on scholarships for "older-than-average" students. Because you have a legal dependent—your child—you are considered an independent student (your parents are not supporting you).

There are a number of government programs for which you may also qualify: Pell Grants, Direct Loans, Federal Supplemental Educational Opportunity Grants, Work Study, and Federal Perkins Loans. All of these government grants and loans require you to fill out a Free Application for Federal Student Aid, or FAFSA, providing information about your income. These forms are available at any high school, junior or community college, or university financial aid office. Most single moms will tell you there is nothing good about being poor, but there is one good thing—you will qualify for just about everything in the way of financial aid based on need as long as you have a high school diploma or GED.

Financial aid programs assess your need by looking at your most recently filed income tax returns. Keep these, photocopy them and file them—just don't throw them away, because you will need them to fill out financial aid forms. If these forms seem complicated, they really aren't. You can even call 1-800-4-FED-AID and get help filling them out. The call is free, and any questions you might have will be answered. Most junior colleges and universities also have people who can help you fill out and file financial aid statements if you have kept all of your records, so you will want to keep and photocopy the following:

- federal and state income tax returns
- child care bills or receipts
- your W-2 form
- alimony or child support records
- medical expense records
- tax returns filed by your former spouse if you are divorced

(Talk this one over with a counselor at the college.)

After you have gathered all of this information you will be ready to start filling out forms. Keep in mind that most single mothers qualify for a lot of financial aid. *Be sure to meet all deadlines. There are NO exceptions.*

We have listed some of the most common types of financial aid grants and loans. In the appendix we have also listed financial aid offices for individual states as well as some scholarships we know of for women or older-than-average students.

Grants and Loans

Loans must be repaid, usually at a low interest rate, after graduation, or completion of education. Grants do not have to be repaid, and the federal government offers two: Pell Grants and Federal Supplemental Educational Opportunity Grants.

To apply for federal grants and loans, go to the financial aid department at the junior college, college, or university you want to attend and pick up an application form, or call 1-800-4-FED-AID and have them send you the ones you want. In general, you will have to prove financial need, which is based on a very simple formula: cost of tuition minus family income equals financial need. It's that easy. If you have any questions, like how to list child support, call 1-800-4-FED-AID and they will help you.

Pell Grants

Administered by the government, this is one of the biggest educational grant programs. It is based on need and a financial aid form must be filled out, but when you fill out a standardized federal financial aid form you automatically apply for the Pell Grant. Remember, single mothers are usually at the low end of the income scale. For once this will be helpful. The amounts of money available are dependent upon congressional appropriations, which change frequently. Check your local library for current information.

Many schools will also have grants that they can give at their own discretion. Ask about them and apply for those as well.

Stafford Loans

These are secured or guaranteed student loans at low interest rates. Five or six months after you stop going to school you usually have to start to repay them. The amounts of the loans vary. As a freshman you can borrow up to $2,625, as a sophmore $3,500, and as a junior, senior, or graduate student up to $5,500 per year. After you stop going to school you usually have to start to repay them.

Perkins Loans

These are also low-cost loans. Usually the interest rate is very low and they have the longest payback time (up to ten years). Undergraduates may borrow $3,000 per year for up to five years, while graduates may borrow $5,000 per year. Total Perkins debts may not exceed $30,000 for undergrad and graduate school combined. You must start to repay them after graduation, just as you do the Stafford Loans.

Education: Your Best Bet

Before you think getting more education is just some "pie in the sky" idea, remember the new welfare reform laws. Without question, education is your best bet. We would never tell you this will be easy, but it is "do-able." In the future, single mothers will be getting little assistance from the government in the form of welfare so take advantage of educational opportunities while you can. As we suggested in Chapter 2, you may want to start with a junior college to keep costs down, but *start.*

Check out any college or junior college carefully. Most junior colleges have day care centers as well, so you can study and meet day care problems in one spot. When asking about day-care programs and also ask about the following:

- Is the university, college, or school accredited?
- What is its refund policy? (If your class is canceled, can you get your money back?)
- What is the job placement rate for the program in which you are interested?
- Does the school offer financial aid? Does it participate in the federal financial aid program? (Some do not.)

Finding Help When You Need It

One of the surest ways of escaping poverty is by getting more education or training. That is true, but for one reason or another many women will not be able to do that immediately. For all too many women it is a struggle to just survive.

How can you feed your son, find shelter and a job, and stay off the streets? For women entering poverty due to an emergency like the death of their spouse, or escaping an abusive home situation, it may be difficult to know where to turn.

Any woman in an abusive relationship can call a womens' shelter. Sometimes it will be called Women's Shelter, or Center Against Rape and Domestic Violence, or the Battered Women's Shelter. Call 911 in your city or town; the operator will know what it is called in your area. Or you can call any social worker and she or he will know how to direct you. These centers are wonderful and will help any woman in need. They will get you started or put you in contact with agencies that will help you find housing, a job, and a day care center, and provide support through the transitional stages toward becoming an independent woman.

If you are not in an abusive situation you can still call the center and ask what kinds of services are available in your area. Also, any social worker will know what services are available and the best way to connect you with them. Don't be afraid to ask questions, and don't hestitate to pick up a phone book and look under city and county social services. The United Way sponsors Transitional Programs for Women and a number of other community outreach programs. You will find a national listing for the United Way in our appendix. Call that number or your local United Way office and ask about community outreach programs they have in your town or city. They will tell you what kinds of services are available for someone with your needs. We will give you a rough idea of some of the services available in most cities and towns.

WIC

WIC is the Women, Infants, and Children Nutrition Program. This program is designed to ensure good nutrition for children under five years of age and their mothers. Mothers and children under five are given food vouchers for formula, milk, cheese, eggs, peanut butter, and other basic foods. It is by no means everything you need, but it is a help. WIC programs are usually run through the county and state, and almost every state has one. Check the phone book to see where your local office is located.

Head Start

If your children are young, Head Start is a wonderful solution to a number of problems single moms face. Head Start will give your child two nutritious meals a day—breakfast and lunch—low-cost day care, the opportunity to play with other children, and he will learn something as well. Whether you're working or going to school, Head Start is an opportunity for your child and yourself. You won't want to miss out on this one. Call your local Head Start office and apply.

Social Services

Check into the social services available to you, if you haven't already. Start by calling your local Aid to Dependent Children (ADC) office. The people there will tell you more about what services are available in your county and help you check into meeting the needs of your children. Ask what kind of help is available on a short-term basis, and possibly longer, for these necessities:

food (food stamps, food banks, or food share programs)
shelter (battered wive's shelters, homeless family shelters, or
assistance with housing, such as first and last month's rent)

clothing (for mothers and children, groups such as the St.
Vincent DePaul Society, Operation School Clothes, or Fresh
Start for Women)
job training, education, or job interview training
child care (Head Start and day care services)
mentoring programs for mother and son

Transitional Programs for Women

One of the main reasons women become homeless is domestic
violence. When this is occurring, for her own safety and that of
her son, a mother probably will not want her son's father
involved in his life. Any woman facing that situation should seek
out a women's shelter immediately. A Centers for Women and
Victims of Domestic Violence (sometimes called a Battered
Women's Shelter) offer a wide range of services to women. First,
they offer you a safe place to stay with your child or children.
Then they can offer help with everything from finding jobs and
housing to services like transportation and relocation. In short,
they can help a woman rebuild her life.

One woman who used the Transitional Program for Women
wrote this thank you letter, giving us a clear picture of what
programs like this can help accomplish.

Dear TPW:
I would like to thank you for all the help I have received
from your program over the past year. The services and
individual attention I got were tremendously beneficial and
I am grateful that this program has been available to me.
Specifically I would like to thank the people that have
helped and supported me in this time of transition (my case
manager, counselor, program director), and all of the Battered Women's Shelter staff.
When I began the TPW program in December 1989, I was
surprised at how much help I needed for me and my family.

As a newly single mother with two young children, I was anxious to find housing, work, and get my emotional and financial life together. Everywhere I turned there were big walls in my way and the resourcefulness of the TPW staff and their guidance and support gave me confidence to continue toward my goal. From the beginning I did not qualify for any aid to dependent families or food stamps due to having a new car (that was not outright mine). I, therefore, had little money, no possessions, and a great need to get my life together. My case manager sat with me weekly going over monthly budgeting, housing, job searches, goal setting, and helping me find food for my family. She has been a wonderful resource for me by getting me in touch with people who have helped me:

- write a resume
- find someone who would rent to an unemployed person
- get a job
- receive food baskets during the holidays
- locate furnishings for my house
- find child care
- increase my parenting skills

Not only was [name of my case manager] resourceful, she also came through at times of crisis and was insightful in what I should really expect from my particular situation. I continue to see her on an irregular basis—maybe once a month. I have also received counseling on a weekly basis and still continue to do so. This service is also invaluable to me, as I feel I am steadily growing in my emotional health.

Each aspect of the program was beneficial and seemed to grow as my needs grew too. People are impressed when I let them know all that the TPW program has done for me. Again, I want to thank the TPW staff for their dedication and support.

Respectfully,

Clairice

Clairice's story is common. All types of women—rich and poor, black and white, doctors and women who never graduated from high school—have used programs like this. They share the experiences that bring them into the Transitional Program for Women or the Battered Women's Shelter. You can see from her letter the kind of help she received and support she felt just by making one phone call.

Even if you are not the victim of domestic violence, the women working at these centers can help you find the kind of help and services you may need, and you should not hesitate to give them a call. They may be known by different names, like Battered Women's Shelter or Center Against Domestic Violence or just the Women's Shelter, but they will be listed in the phone book or you can call any county agency and they will give you the name and number for the services in your area.

Clothing

There are a number of agencies that will help you and your children with clothing. The Junior League (listed in the appendix) runs a number of programs in almost every city in the country to help provide new or like-new clothing for needy families. They can provide mothers with clothing for starting a job and children with school clothes. In many places they also provide mentors or other women who will establish a friendship with you and help you with skills like preparing for job interviews or other situations.

Job Interviews

Under the new welfare reform laws most people will actually be given a class in preparing for a job interview. It will teach you what to say, how to improve your chances of getting a job, and what an employer considers good work habits that are necessary to keep a job. Many other groups also offer help specifically for women in transition. In many cities the Junior League has a mentoring program for women. Check with social services to see what groups in your community offer services like this to help women through transition.

Collecting Child Support

If you are on public assistance, the agency will ask for the identity of your child's father so the state can try to collect child support for you. Frequently mothers are working and still impoverished because they are not receiving child support. If you are on welfare, the Association for Children for Enforcement of Support, commonly called ACES, is an agency that may help you. With over three hundred chapters, ACES is one of the largest national groups dedicated to helping children receive the support they need. We have listed the main office in the appendix, but you can call the office nearest to your home and it will help.

If you are a victim of domestic violence, you may feel it is too dangerous to try to collect child support from the child's father. Even the state and the federal government recognize the danger mothers and children can be in under these circumstances and allowances are made.

Health and Nutrition

Perhaps the most important key to good health and nutrition is having enough food. We realize that for many single mothers and their children there isn't enough food. We hope we have given you some ideas on where to go for assistance if you need food. Start with the Women's, Infants, and Children Nutrition Program. People at WIC are usually trained nutritionists who have good ideas on stretching your food dollars. They also offer basic nutrition lessons and information to help you and your children have the best nutrition possible. Also remember the Head Start program, it gives children two meals a day, and that is a big help. We will mention a few ways to help you stretch your food dollars as well.

According to new nutritional guides, the healthiest diets have a higher percentage of grains and starches and lower amounts of red meats. It is also important to eat three to five fruits or vegetables a day. For anyone on a limited budget this is good news, because the reduction in red meats and dairy products is also a reduction in the most expensive part of the food budget. Casseroles and stir fry dishes are excellent ways to stretch small amounts of meat and include larger portions of grains like rice, pasta, or noodles. Casseroles, stir fries, and one-dish skillet meals all accomplish these goals.

Some single mothers move into then out of poverty. It isn't easy for women to escape, but it can be done, and help is available if you know where to go. We hope we have given you ideas on where to start looking, and there is a lot more information in the appendix of this book, where you will find numbers to call. Don't be afraid to call, and don't hesitate to ask questions.

7

Abuse and the Single Mother

Domestic violence is one of the most important subjects related to single motherhood. Every year this American tragedy touches women of all socio-economic classes, forcing them to uproot their everyday lives and flee for safety—their own and their child's. It is one of the main reasons middle-class and upper-middle class women are thrown into poverty, unable to obtain child support, and forced to banish their children's fathers from their lives.

Women tell us they have had to take their children and flee from their homes, leaving everything behind. The lucky ones ran to a relative's home, but many do not because they fear they will put that family member in danger as well, or that the abusive partner will know where to find them. Sometimes they are without food, money, and shelter, and by necessity they become single mothers. When a battered woman and child are hiding it is too dangerous to collect child support. The result is instant poverty for mother and son.

While pediatricians and family practicioners have been aware of child abuse for a long time, they now know that abused children are one product of an abusive home. The abused woman is usually the other. The problem is now so prevelent one doctor

115

routinely asks his patients, "Are you safe in your home?" And "Is everyone in your family safe at home?"

Dr. Harry Rinehart explains his approach in his community-based clinic: "The reason people don't tell doctors about domestic violence is that doctors don't ask. When we do ask no one is offended that we raised the issue. We approach the topic of domestic violence with the same attitude. If it is a problem, let's do something about it. If it is not a problem, no offense intended."

Child Abuse

Physical child abuse involves a physical assault on a child or failure to protect the child from nonaccidental injury requiring medical attention or legal intervention. Young children cannot protect themselves. It is up to parents to protect them and see to it that children are safe when the parents must be away.

In the United States the incidence of child abuse and domestic violence is extraordinarily high. In 1993 the U.S. Advisory Board on Child Abuse and Neglect reported that more than 2.5 million children were maltreated.[1] Everyone should be concerned about child abuse, as parents of children and tax-paying providers of health services to children.

Abuse and Neglect

Michael

Michael is a two-year-old boy who lives with his mother and her live-in companion. His mother works full-time as a waitress, earning $4.75 per hour—less than a living wage. The family relocated to a new apartment in a low-income area along with the mother's live-in male companion, who was not Michael's biological father. He was unemployed, had a police record, and alcohol and drug problems. He was caring for Michael while the mother was at work when the boy soiled his pants. The mother's boyfriend, thinking that Michael was stubborn and deliberately disobedient by not taking care of himself in the toilet, became very angry and put the boy in a tub of scalding hot water. Michael screamed with pain, and the man took him out of the tub.

When Michael's mother returned home her son was still in much distress. She saw that he was scalded, and she immediately took him to the hospital emergency room. There the doctor treated Michael's burns, telling his mother that they were probably "nonaccidental." The physician called protective services, initiating an investigation and the filing of criminal charges against her live-in boyfriend.

On a day when the mother thought that she did everything "right," her world seemed to fall apart. She went to work, leaving her child with a friend she trusted. Her companion totally misread her little boy's behavior and punished him in a way that injured him. The mother started the day as a single parent with serious financial problems and ended the day with all those problems, plus a traumatized, injured son and a male companion with big legal problems.

The Risks for Sons

A question we are often asked is: "Why are sons at risk because they are raised by a single parent? If a woman is competent and caring, why can't she raise a child effectively by herself?"

All things being equal, many single parents provide effective and caring homes for their children, but Michael's mother faced too many problems before she was mature enough to handle them all. After her brief marriage ended, she and her child became poor, were forced to move to a new neighborhood, and became isolated from friends and family. Perhaps because she was lonely and too trusting—or naive—she befriended a male who made her situation much worse. Michael's mother was poor, overworked, isolated, and had few social supports, leaving precious little time for the day-to-day parenting that helps young boys and girls develop emotionally and intellectually. Her son became part of an all-too familiar statistic. In about 90 percent of cases of confirmed child abuse the child was abused by a family member or someone known to the family.

Michael's Perspective

By age two, Michael had the kind of personal experiences capable of distorting his image of what it is to be a male. His biological father deserted the family, leaving him to be raised by his stressed mother. His second "father figure" hurt him for nothing more than behaving like the two-year-old he was. He learned some horrendous ideas about adult male behavior through direct experience. These images of how males act when angry or abandon relationships can outlast the serious wounds he suffered from the scalding.

How children react to abuse in a family depends on the intensity and frequency of that abuse. Common long-term problems, which usually outlast the physical injuries, include speech and language problems, school difficulties, and delinquency. Adults who were abused or neglected in childhood have a higher rate of criminal behavior and marital and child-rearing problems.[2]

What Can You Do to Protect Your Child From Abuse?

Ask yourself the question, "Is your child safe in your home?" He probably is, but pose the question anyway. If you are unwilling to think about the question you will not be able to prevent a problem before it happens.

Are you, for whatever reason, so stressed that you might overreact and hurt your child when you try to correct or discipline him? Is your spouse or companion stressed and likely to overreact to the child's behavioral problems? Are you uncertain about how to discipline your child? Do you feel angry or upset long after your child misbehaves? If you answer yes, ask for help. One way is to call your physician and seek an appointment for your child—even a well-child checkup. If your physician does not ask you the question, "Is everyone in your family safe"—tell him your concerns. Some ministers are also very well informed about community resources and can offer assistance.

Sexual Abuse and Your Child

Child sexual abuse is a form of rape. A child victim is not capable of full and informed consent. Children who experience sexual abuse suffer, and the meaning of the abuse changes as they get older.[3] Some teenagers who have been sexually abused by a family member leave home because they believe being homeless and on the streets is safer than remaining at home. Other children who are sexually abused adopt immoral sexual values and carry them forward to the next generation.

One example of an immoral value is to view sex not as an expression of love and intimacy, but as a way of obtaining favors. This distorted view of sexuality may explain why a substantial number of prostitutes have histories of childhood sexual abuse. Sexually abused boys are much more likely to carry forward the idea that sex is exploitation.[4] They may grow up to abuse others, or they may not feel good about their sexuality.

Who Sexually Abuses Children?

Women very rarely sexually molest children. Statistics based on confirmed abuse incidents indicate that approximately 97 to 98 percent of child sexual abuse offenders are male.[5] Of course, the majority of men do not sexually molest children, but the vast majority of molesters are male.

Men who sexually abuse children do so consistent with their sexual orientation. Heterosexual males who sexually abuse children target girls often between eight and ten years of age. The male perpetrator is usually twenty or more years older than his victim, and he is usually someone the family knows:[6] Stepfathers and live-in companions of the mother are more frequently abusers than are biological fathers.

Men who abuse boys are usually homosexual; however, homosexual males are not more likely than heterosexuals to abuse children.

A boy is more likely than a girl to be abused by a stranger, which is a special concern when income and family problems cause a single parent with boys to move to a high-risk neighborhood where they are without friends or relatives they can trust.

Victims of Sexual Abuse

Boys and girls suffer physical abuse and neglect in about equal numbers, although our daughters are much more likely to be victims of *sexual* abuse than our sons. (About five times as many girls are victims of sexual abuse as boys.) However, a boy who is a victim may be at a special disadvantage: He may wonder why he was "selected" as a target, and even think the perpetrator believed that he was homosexual.[7]

Boys have a harder time sharing their feelings, and they are less likely than girls to confide or tell anyone about the abuse. If a boy keeps his abuse a secret it may occur again and again. Furthermore, keeping the abuse to himself will also keep him from getting help and counseling.[8]

What Can You Do to Prevent Child Sexual Abuse?

1. Become familiar with symptoms of child sexual abuse.
There is no one way that children show the effects of sexual

abuse. Children who have been abused may show these in different ways. Some abused children display emotional problems such as nightmares, fear of places or certain people, or changes in appetite or sleep patterns. An abused child may engage in sexual activity with other children and may "know" more about sexual behavior than other children of the same age. Still others become aggressive, abuse alcohol or drugs, or show truancy and loss of interest in school.

What follows is a list of symptoms shown by children who have been victimized by sexual abuse. It has been provided by two psychologists, David A. Wolfe and Vicky V. Wolfe, who have substantial experience in treating abused children.[9]

Common Signs and Symptoms Exhibited by Sexual Abuse Victims

Undercontrolled Behaviors
aggressiveness, hostility, disruptiveness
chronic running away
alcohol and/or drug abuse
compulsive lying
truancy, decline in school performance

Overcontrolled Behaviors
crying for no apparent reason
fears associated with particular places or persons
withdrawal from peers
self-regulation problems (sleep, appetite, appearance, weight gain or loss)
regressive behaviors (thumb sucking, bed wetting)

Sexual Behaviors and Physical Complaints
age-inappropriate sexual acting out
vague physical complaints
precocious sexual language or knowledge
overt seductive behavior

fear of touching or being touched
prostitution

The above list is based on confirmed cases of sexual abuse, many of which reached the courts after abuse occurred a number of times over many years. As a parent you want to prevent abuse, but if it occurs you want help for your child before he or she becomes desperate and is truant from school, runs away from home, or engages in promiscuity or prostitution.

Early warning signs of sexual abuse are not specific to sexual abuse alone. For example, a child who is upset may act fearful toward particular places or persons, withdraw from friends, cry, or be anxious. A child may react this way for any number of reasons, such as losing a good friend in a move, or being teased, upset, or disappointed about something.

Because signs of sexual abuse are nonspecific until the abuse is chronic, it is crucial that your child feels comfortable in telling you when bad things happen to him. You will need information from your child about what is wrong, and for this to happen he needs to know that he can talk to you about his worries even when they are embarrassing.

2. Keep communication between you and your child open.
Most sexually abused children find it difficult to tell their parent or some other adult about the abuse, but boys find it harder than girls to talk to a parent about it. This should not be a surprise. We, as adults, often find it difficult to confide our troubles as well, which is why a growing number of physicians will ask a patient, "Are you safe in your home?" Physicians want to make it clear that it is okay for their patients to talk to them about domestic violence, and they will help if there is a problem.

When your child is old enough to understand, but by all means by age seven, explain to your youngster that sexual contact between himself and an older child or an adult is wrong. Tell him what you mean by sexual contact or behavior in words he will comprehend. You may say no one should be allowed to touch his private parts—or penis. Make it very clear that if someone even suggests such a thing, he should refuse and tell you.

This basic and straightforward talk has helped some children get out of a difficult situation, and has helped many confide in a parent.

3. Check out programs that serve children and be sure they are safe.

There are substantial advantages and opportunities for your child to be involved in Boy Scouts, a Sunday school program, or summer youth program. Because isolated cases of child molestation have occurred in some of these, most have taken steps to prevent abuse. Ask if the program requires what is called a volunteer disclosure statement from every adult who will have contact with children. The following are examples of questions that may be asked of those who are hired—or volunteer—to work with children.

Volunteer Disclosure Form

History (Please answer yes or no—attach explanation for each yes.)

a. Have you every been convicted for possession, use, or sale of drugs?
b. Have you been convicted of a crime against children or other persons?
c. Within the past year have you abused alcohol, or legal or illegal drugs?

Disclosure forms also list what is expected of a paid employee—or volunteer—who will have contact with children. Usually the person is required to sign the written form and agree to a background check.

Domestic Violence: Mother as Victim

When Martha had overspent her Visa account her husband struck her in the face with his fist. She was afraid and called 911, but she later withdrew her complaint and explained that she was at fault because she had provoked her husband by her careless spending habits. Several more attacks "happened," and she excused them all. Her husband had a good income and she was reluctant to leave her share of it. Finally, her eight-year-old son called 911 when a "family dispute" became a physical assault that injured her one more time. She asked herself, "Should I assume the blame again and let my son believe that it's okay for a husband to beat his wife to settle an argument?" She filed a complaint and went to a shelter with her son.

If you or your child are the victim of domestic violence, go to a battered women's shelter.

Domestic Violence Carried Forward: When Boys Get in Trouble

Boys express problems in ways widely different from the ways girls express them. Troubled teenage girls develop anorexia nervosa about twenty times as often as teenage boys, and adolescent girls are about twice as likely to develop clinical depression as are adolescent boys. Boys, in turn, perhaps because of greater impulsiveness, commit suicide about four times as often as girls.

Let's consider two mental health conditions that occur predominantly in one gender and not the other: anorexia nervosa among teenage girls and aggressive, antisocial behavior among adolescent and teenage boys.

Anorexia nervosa is a serious eating disorder which occurs in about 1 in 250 females, usually between the ages of twelve and eighteen. An individual with this disorder shows an intense fear of becoming obese, experiences significant weight loss, and refuses to maintain a minimal healthy body weight.[10] This person may believe that she is fat, even when emaciated, and gaze at the mirror while being concerned about imagined obesity. Many times these adolescent girls need to be hospitalized to prevent starvation, but even with hospitalization, about 15 to 20 percent of these patients die from complications of the condition.

These girls are often described as perfectionists and model children. Characteristically they will vigorously deny that they have an illness, and essentially never refer themselves for treatment.[11] Their problem is noticed by parents or teachers, or during routine medical exams.

While concern about physical appearance and dress may well be consistent with an image of femininity, an obsession with thinness when it compromises health distorts the sense of being a woman. So, too, does a preoccupation with perfectionism, especially when it leads to passivity.

Fatherless Sons and Aggressive Behavior

On average, boys raised in single-parent families show more aggressive and antisocial behavior than do sons raised in two-parent families. Research shows, however, that the sex of the custodial parent has little to do with the child's adjustment. Boys raised by single-parent fathers are not better adjusted, on average, than boys raised by a mother,[12] though fathers who are single parents tend to earn more money than women and their higher incomes offer advantages. But when you rule out income, children do equally well with a mother's or father's custody. A single parent who is able to provide a loving, stable family environment and is economically secure can raise a child successfully. It is the softer stuff of parenting, rather than sex of the parent, that makes a difference.

While boys express problems differently than girls (and are more likely to be aggressive), they can be raised successfully by a single parent of either gender. Often the problems shown by these boys start with seemingly normal but difficult behavior and then gradually develop into seriously aggressive behavior. We believe these boys develop a distorted view of what it is like to be male or masculine, creating problems for themselves and the rest of us. Let's look at the problems Tony faced as he grew up and became aggressive.

A Distorted Sense of Masculinity

Tony

    Tony is a sixteen-year-old boy who has exhibited behavioral problems since he was a preschooler. As a young boy he had problems shown by most boys and girls to a varying degree. He was impatient and had rather frequent temper tantrums at home, at school, and in restaurants, but his behavior was not considered a problem prior to starting school.

    By the time he was in second grade his behavior became more of a problem. He fought on the playground and a teacher had to monitor his behavior and from time to time send him to the principal's office for being disruptive. He fell far behind in his academic work, was often angry, and displayed little self-restraint in expressing it.

    When he became an adolescent his mother began to fear him because of his frequent outbursts and pulled back from close supervision and discipline. She stopped asking him where he was going for weekend events or insisting on an agreed-upon time for him to be home. His father was not involved in his parenting except for two or three contacts a year.

    As Tony entered his fourteenth year he was physically stronger and "tougher" than most boys his age. Sometimes he assaulted boys for no other reason than to show everyone how tough he was. If provoked he felt he had an "obligation" to get even and be physically aggressive.

He became sexually active and forced a girlfriend into sexual activity when she did not want sex. The girl became pregnant, and Tony told a friend that he got her pregnant so she "wouldn't fool around." Tony expanded his pattern of antisocial behavior. He entered and burglarized a house, was caught, and now has a juvenile court record.

Signs of a Distorted Male Image

A boy with a distorted male image, like Tony's could be described in any of the following ways:

- He shows little capacity to empathize with others and he violates the rights of others.
- He acts as if aggression and intimidation against others is okay when it satisfies his immediate wants.
- He misinterprets the behavior of others and often incorrectly believes he is provoked.
- While he may believe that his sexual prowess and aggressive behavior is normal, his conduct is flagrantly exploitative.

Adolescent boys commit violent acts that get them in trouble with the law about fifty times more often than girls do.[13] While doing so, these young men show that they are failing to develop adult values of acceptable male behavior, namely to live in a way that fosters a committed relationship with a spouse, be a caring parent for sons and daughters, and resolve differences without aggression.

We want to stress that hyper-aggressive behavior in boys is not a sign of high self-esteem, nor is it a sign of strength. Boys and girls who are emotionally strong and have good self-esteem show it with a capacity for patience, diligence, endurance, and persistence. They also show self-esteem and emotional strength by a willingness to express empathy for others and to handle problems with understanding rather than by impulsively acting out in anger. Superior work habits are also a sign of strength. Very aggressive boys, in contrast, often display little persistence, get bored easily, and want immediate gratification of their needs.

However, there is a similarity between girls who develop anorexia nervosa and boys who become violent and antisocial. Girls who are affected by this condition adamantly deny they have a problem, and denial is also universal among aggressive and delinquent boys. It is up to parents and teachers to notice that a boy's behavior is crossing a line and that at risk to self-destruct and become a hazard to others in society.

Nathan McCall, author of *Makes Me Wanna Holler*, relates his experiences growing up and gradually turning from a promising young student to one who lost interest in school and joined a group of alienated boys who each got into serious trouble with the law by assaulting blacks and whites, both male and female.[14]

He says that his behavior, and the behavior of the other boys in his group, did not seem wrong at the time. "Ever since I could recall, I and everybody else I knew had associated manhood with physical dominance and conquest of someone else."

Teenage boys who attack other youths were often aggressive at age seven, and men who are abusive to their wives were also aggressive by the same age. When a boy becomes established as an aggressive person he comes to believe that his aggression is justified.

If we are to save our sons from violence and gangs, we must start by teaching them to deal with anger and conflicts by talking and not using force or violence, and this has to start around the age of seven. Remember Nathan McCalls words: "Ever since I can remember...."[15]

8

Finding Positive
Male Role Models

Single mothers often find it difficult to find positive male role models for their sons. Extensive research tells us that young men need an older male to help them understand and "demonstrate" what it means to become a man.[1] For centuries fathers have filled this role, but many mothers find their sons's father either unwilling, unavailable, and in some cases unfit to fill the role. What can mothers do to help their sons develop a positive male image and learn behaviors that will help them live productive, successful, happy, and emotionally stable lives?

There are a number of things mothers can do to provide their sons with a positive male role, and they can start with their own families. Are there male relatives who can pick up some of the slack? Does your son have a grandfather, uncle, or older male cousin who is a positive role model and can be trusted? If so, start by including that male in family activities. Invite your dad to dinner or to a special outing with your son.

However, you may want to consider how much responsibility to give this family member. Some mothers feel comfortable with a casual arrangement with relatives and are happy to have their sons go with Grandpa or "brother" whenever and wherever possible. Other women find they want a well-defined under-standing with family members as to where their sons will go, what activities they will do, and when they will be home. They may fear their brothers or fathers may grow too close to their sons and will be unable to let go when she becomes involved in a committed relationship with another man who may wish to assume the role of father. But for some boys relatives provide a caring role model when it is needed most, as seen in Keith's and Peter's experience.

Keith

When the fifth-grade class had a father and son dinner at school, one recently widowed mother called her father and asked him if he would take her eleven-year-old son Keith. Grandpa was happy to step in, and although her son missed his dad, he was glad he wasn't left out of his class activity.

Peter

Although from a stable and close-knit family herself, Lanna wasn't as lucky in marriage. Her husband left her when their son, Peter, was only two months old. From the time he was little, Lanna's brother, Joe, started including Lanna's son in activities with his own family. Joe took Peter on hunting trips, to baseball games, and to the park with his own kids. He also took part in Peter's school activities whenever needed.

Mentoring

Sometimes there isn't a male family member available. Male family members may be too far away, deceased, or unable or unfit to take part in your son's life. When a positive male role model isn't available in her own family, what can a mother do to provide her son with someone who can help him achieve manhood in the best sense of the word?

Mentoring programs are one of the best solutions. Mentoring is a proven way to help a young man fill the gap in his life left by an absent father.

What Is Mentoring?

Mentoring is a one-on-one relationship between a mentor (an experienced person) and a mentee (sometimes a child, an adolescent, or even a mother) in which the mentor will hopefully, be able to pass some of his or her experience on to the mentee. Mentors acts as a teachers, resource persons, or advocates. They become friends who can listen. Mentors almost always act as role models. They encourage and build the self-confidence of mentees, and in doing so may change the lives of the people they are mentoring.

Mentor programs are very successful in helping young people turn their lives around, but they are also helpful in helping women become more skilled mothers and more successful people. Lets look at some of the different types of mentoring and mentoring programs.

Five Kinds of Mentoring

Laura Foley, director of Mentoring Works, a mentoring program that matches mentors with mentees in Oregon, breaks down mentoring into five basic types:

- traditional
- long-term focused activity
- short-term focused activity
- team mentoring
- group mentoring

Traditional

Traditional programs are what most of us know of when we talk about mentoring: Big Brothers and Big Sisters, Partners, and a number of others. We think of the Big Brothers and Big Sisters programs for good reason: It is perhaps one of the best-known and most successful examples of traditional mentoring. Partners, another outstanding example, is also becoming very popular nationwide. Information and applications for both programs are available through your local YMCA.

Traditional programs usually require a long-term commitment of at least a year of the mentor (the adult) and the mentee (the youth or mother) to a one-on-one relationship. Mentors are carefully screened, and then matched with a youth. The mentor's role is not to take the child to expensive places or buy fancy gifts, but to act as a friend, listener, and role model while doing "fun" activities together. Sometimes they play ball, or go fishing, or to a school game.

Long-Term Focused Activity

Again, this is a one-on-one program as well, but with a strong focus on one area, like academics. Education Commission of the States, YES, Project Peace, and Hands-on Science Outreach, Inc., are all examples of long-term focused mentoring programs. More information on these programs can be found in the appendix of this book.

Aimed at school success and improving long-term career outcomes, this type of program uses mentors as tutors and career models as well as friends. Mentors are screened and there is a major focus on matching the skills, interests, and career objectives of mentor and mentee. Frequently mentors will go through a training program, and they must be willing to make a commitment of six hours a month for at least a year. Activities are centered around school and academic programs, and a more personal relationship is left to both the mentor and mentee.

This kind of program is also closely supervised. School guidance counselors can usually refer you to programs like this, but so can churches, youth counselors, and social service agencies.

Short-Term Focused Activity

In many ways this is similar to a long-term focused program. These mentors are tutors and they encourage a student in academic endeavors, but there is more of a short-term commitment for mentor and mentee. Outward Bound and Breakthrough are two examples that focus on wilderness experiences for boys. Some other examples might be summer internships or science or computer "camps," like those conducted by Hands-on Science Outreach, Inc., or the Safe Kids/Safe Neighborhoods programs around the country that teach job training and peer leadership skills. The program and the needs of the mentee may determine the relationship the mentor and the mentee have, but it is always one of encouragement on the part of the mentor. He may take the mentee to work with him or he could be involved in classroom activity with the mentee.

Team Mentoring

In this situation a family "adopts" a youth (usually from a single-parent family) and invites him to family activities. The most well-known and widely available example of this type of program is House of Umoja. Families are screened thoroughly, and a match is based on things like the interests of mentor and mentee, location, and personalities of everyone involved. Because the mentee becomes part of an extended family, he has a chance to experience, firsthand, a functioning family as they solve problems, work together, and interact as a family. As with most mentoring programs, this one requires a long-term commitment so the child can form a bond with the family and they with him.

Group Mentoring

This is the type of program we are all familiar with and many of us have experienced. Boy Scouts, 4-H, and Camp Fire are all examples of group mentoring. Sports programs like Little League and the American Youth Soccer Organization (AYSO) also fall into this category. Usually there is one adult and a group of youngsters. Screening is not as extensive but training is usually more so. A mentor makes a long-term commitment and meets with the group on a regular basis. Activities are usually structured group activities, and in many situations the program and the group, rather than the mentor, can have a bigger impact on the youth. Sometimes this type of mentoring is not enough for a child who needs more one-on-one with a male adult, but it can be a wonderful addition to a child's life if he already has a grandfather, uncle, or other male figure but needs more.

What You Need to Know

Most mentoring programs are free. Schools, social agencies, and even the courts can refer you to one, and you can refer yourself by calling the local Boys and Girls Club, YMCA, or even juvenile courts and ask them for the names and numbers of any local mentoring groups.

You should ask some questions and find out as much as possible about the program you're interested in before you refer your son to it. Here are some of the questions you will want to pose:

- Do you do background checks on mentors?
- Do these include criminal checks through the Department of Human Resources?

- Do mentors attend workshops or educational programs?
- What do you expect of parents in the program and mentees?
- What are the goals your group works on?
- How are they matched with mentees?
- How closely are they supervised?
- What kind of time commitment will be involved for the mentor and your son?
- Is there follow-up?

It is easy to see why you would want to ask the first few questions. Obviously, you do not want someone working with your child who is a convicted felon or a child molester. We found the really good programs do a number of things, from screening mentors carefully to putting them through criminal checks (up to five times) using the Department of Human Resources (DHR). Sometimes the check process includes an interview and questionnaire asking if the person has ever used illegal drugs, been arrested, etc. These answers are checked through the DHR for truthfulness as well as any hidden criminal history. References, fingerprints, and past jobs and living situations are checked. Then the potential mentor is put through still another interview. The program trains mentors and provides ongoing workshops and educational programs. There is always supervision, and mentors meet monthly with directors and other mentors to answer questions that might pop up and to work out problems.

Good programs also require a long term commitment from the mentor and the mentee so the child can form a bond with the mentor. A worthwhile program will also follow up with you and your child. They will call from time to time to see how things are going long after the crisis has passed. Hopefully, if your child has a good mentor relationship the mentor will be in his life for a long time.

Last, but by no means least, worthwhile programs look at the child in his family and the environment in which he lives. If possible, they help the mother and siblings as well.

Lucas: A Success Story

Fifteen-year-old Lucas did not enter his mentoring program willingly. He was strongly urged into it (forced, really) by his mother and an arresting officer after he was caught wearing gang colors and spraying graffiti on the wall of a local business. He begged his mother to "buy" him out of the situation, but on the advice of the high school counselor, she decided that a mentoring program might be her best chance to save her son from the suburban gang with whom he naively flirted.

His mother was a good mother. She went to church on a regular basis and took the kids. She thought she was doing everything right, everything she knew how to do. Her job paid well, but it took time away from Lucas, and like most people living in the suburbs, she wasn't even aware that gangs are now a middle-class problem no longer confined to the inner city. While she had "rules" for her son, increasingly she felt she was losing him.

In elementary school, Lucas was considered a bright young man with a lot of talent in sports and science. His teachers were always impressed with his curious mind. He was constantly asking questions and took the time to do high-quality work right up to the ninth grade.

In high school lots of thing started to get to him: He found it was hard to fit in, he wasn't good in sports, and he had difficulty making friends. He wanted to "belong," and the most accepting group consisted of other rejected kids, many of whom were gang "wannabes" who were more than happy to tell him, "you belong with us."

When Lucas was caught "tagging" (spray painting gang-related graffiti), he was referred to a mentoring program by the court and ordered to spend a year meeting with his mentor. He was also placed in a conflict-resolution class in which he learned social skills and how to handle anger and frustration in nonviolent ways. Lucas was referred by the courts, but he got other help as well: He and his mother went to counseling and together they worked on communication.

Lucas met with his mentor once a week for three hours each time. Sometimes they shot hoops; sometimes they did school projects; and once his mentor took him to work with him. Mary also took a class on effective parenting of teens. She realized that parenting a teenager isn't easy for anyone, and it didn't take long before she started to see a difference in her relationship with her son and in his relationship with others. Lucas is in college now, working on a degree.

Lucas's "sentence" did more than keep him out of reform school: It turned his life around. He learned needed social skills and developed interests that helped him make friends. His grades improved and so did his social skills. He learned nonviolent ways to solve problems with other students, and most of all he learned to respect himself and others.

National Programs

There are a number of national programs, listed in the appendix of this book, which you can call for more information. Some inspire a longer description than the appendix would allow, so we will expand on are a few here that are truly noteworthy, diverse, or unknown and greatly deserving of your attention.

Big Brothers/Big Sisters of America

Well-known and highly successful, this program runs in almost every city and state across the country. We listed the phone number for their national office, which you can call to get the address and number of the Big Brothers program in your neighborhood. It is a traditional program consisting of one-on-one mentoring. The activities are informal and the mentor is a friend, listener, and confidence builder.

Mentors are screened carefully in stages and go through about five checks. After they have been thoroughly checked out they attend an orientation meeting in which they meet other potential mentors and learn about problems that can arise. While this popular program has a waiting list, priority is given to children from single-parent homes between six and sixteen years of age.

A four-year study found that boys who were in the Big Brother program made some real personal gains. They experienced more academic success, had fewer encounters with the police, were not institutionalized, were better able to strengthen family relationships, and took more personal pride in their appearance.[2] You will want to call the Big Brothers Program in your community. In different communities it is run through different agencies, but it always adheres to the national guidelines.

Partners

Partners is another traditional program using the one-on-one formula to serve at-risk youths. Like so many of us, Partners believes that mentoring is an effective way to help children at risk stay away from crime and drugs. This volunteer program, started in Denver, Colorado, has "senior partners" (the mentor) and "junior partners" (the mentee), and tries to help children improve both academically and socially by helping them develop academic, social, and coping skills for life. By improving a child's self-concept, it hopes to reduce his chances of getting into trouble with the law.

This program is truly noteworthy because it comes with support systems in place. There are also monthly group activities, like semi-monthly skills workshops, and health and counseling services. Also, backup services offer significant help for families. Look up this program in the appendix. If there is one near you, you are lucky.

Hands-on Science Outreach, Inc.

This is a program devoted to helping children improve academically by giving them out-of-school science experiences. It is a focused-activity mentoring program that also does small group mentoring on a long-term and short-term basis, and currently operates in twenty-eight states across the country. Its after-school and summer programs help students from four to twelve years improve academically, and in doing so improve their self-concept. These are in the appendix. If your area does not have one of these programs, check the summer science programs that are offered by your school's enrichment programs.

Boy Scouts of America

Everyone has heard of the Boy Scouts. While it is a group mentoring program, what it offers the at-risk young man is worth mentioning. Through structured activities it teaches young men self-reliance and the skills they will need in life, as well as in scouting. Boys learn social skills and character-building values, that are taught and reinforced in a group setting, which provides a good alternative to street gangs.

Camp Fire Boys and Girls

This is also a group mentoring program, but it offers slightly more mentoring at all levels. A coeducational group, Camp Fire offers some academic support and has a one-on-one element in its Career Beginnings program, which matches a student with an adult mentor from the business community. Workshops are also offered. In most cities, Camp Fire Boys and Girls will be listed in the white pages of the phone book. If you can't find a listing, call the office of your child's school. Often the school can supply a local person and number for you to contact.

Mentoring for Mothers

Bonnie: A Mentoring Success

When Bonnie came to the Battered Women's Shelter with her three young sons she was five months pregnant and had just been beaten—again. At first she didn't know if she could leave her husband, a successful and well-known contractor. Bonnie was given a mentor as part of the program, and on her mentor's advice, Bonnie agreed to go for an ultrasound three days before Thanksgiving. Bonnie asked her mentor to come along, and her mentor graciously accepted. Together they learned that Bonnie's unborn baby was dying from kidney and liver failure and Bonnie's life was also in great danger.

Her mentor was able to place all three boys in good homes to be welcomed and cared for during the Thanksgiving holiday and while Bonnie was in the hospital. Sadly, Bonnie's unborn baby died, but Bonnie is alive today because her mentor sought medical care for her. Three young children have the mother they need so badly, and she is a mother who is growing stronger and more confident all the time. Bonnie and her mentor are a true success story.

There are two additional groups worth mentioning that serve mothers and children in need of mentoring.

Family Service of America

This national group works with both mother and child in an effort to strengthen American families. It teaches the kinds of problem-solving skills that are needed in today's families, and works with teen mothers and single mothers to provide other forms of help. It also provides one-on-one mentoring for at-risk youths. We have listed it in the appendix.

The Association of Junior Leagues

We mentioned this group in the previous chapter. Through their community outreach programs, Junior Leagues provide a number of services. The Teen Outreach Program (TOP) helps at-risk youths academically, and sometimes has focused group mentoring to help improve children's academic success. In many locations Junior Leagues offer one-on-one mentoring programs for mothers as well. Mentors also teach skill building, but they focus on parenting, job skills, and interview skills, which so many young mothers need. As in all good mentoring programs, it offers positive role models who listen, teach, and encourage. There is a Junior League in almost every town in the country.

These mentoring programs are just a fraction of what we have listed in the appendix. Mentoring programs can be an enormous catalyst in the life of a young person, a mother, a family, and society. Everyone benefits from mentoring, a good mentor turns lives around, one at a time. We encourage you to look into these programs for your son and yourself. If you need more information, contact the following group:

Educational Resources Information
Center Clearing House
Columbia University
Teachers College, Box 40
New York, NY 10027
(212) 678-3433

IV

•••••

When Everything Goes Well

9

Positive Outcomes

As we reviewed studies about boys raised without a father in the home and interviewed mothers, fathers, and boys—some who are now grown men—it became clear that very successful outcomes did occur. The paths to success differed from one family to another, but some common threads appeared again and again.

In one case adoption provided a very positive outcome for a child whose biological parents were not able to provide a stable and supportive family structure.

In other cases divorce did not result in family breakdown for the children. In such families both the mother and the father—though divorced—remained committed and involved parents for their children. They supported their children's education, and provided consistent discipline and supervision. These successful parents, despite their divorce, maintained contact with relatives and friends and were connected to their community.

These are factors that influence an outcome. We call them protective factors because they help children do well despite their circumstances.

Protective Factors for Children of Divorce

There are factors that help a child through the roughest of times. We have listed, and explained, a few of them.

1. **News of the Divorce:** Divorce is difficult for children because it means the breakdown of the family. It raises many questions and concerns for a child, and discussing these issues will help. Children need to know they will be cared for in a stable family setting, but they may have other concerns as well. Discussing these issues with your child will help him cope.

2. **Father's Involvement:** Having a father remain committed to maintaining a parental role and visitation gives a child security. It is especially helpful when the father is interested and supportive in all aspects of the child's life, including school, as well as other interests and activities the child is involved in. If a man is unable to earn money he may feel excluded from the role of father. In today's world we may need to help fathers understand they can play an important part in their child's life even during periods of unemployment or when they are poor. By staying with the family through hard times and continuing to make an effort to find work, an unemployed father sets a positive example.

3. **Conflict Resolution:** It is important and helpful if the parents agree and support each other on matters concerning the child. A climate of threats, intimidation, or abuse will cancel out other gains.

4. **Stable Enviroment:** Being able to remain in the same neighborhood with established friends is also helpful. Frequent moves add additional stress. Living in a safe neighborhood with few crime problems is also very important.

5. **Effective Discipline:** Children do better if they have parents who discipline effectively and consistently, using (nonviolent) consequences for misbehavior and rewards for positive behavior. It is especially important that a parent

monitor a child and set limits. Parents who know who their children are with, where they are, and what they are doing give them critical guidance and support.

6. **School Performance:** Parents must help their children prepare for school as youngsters by providing learning opportunities. When in school, continued parental interest and support is important in helping a child learn academic and prevocational skills that prepare him for adult life.

7. **Family and Community Support:** When family, friends, relatives, and the community support a child throughout his growing years, he will develop a sense of identity and feel connected to those who care about him.

Escalation Factors for Children of Divorce

There are also factors that make a bad situation much worse and add to the chances that a child will not do well. These include the following:

1. **News of the Divorce:** Poor communication between the parent and child about the divorce and how it will affect him.
2. **Abandonment:** Absence of the father's involvement with the child.
3. **Unresolved Conflicts:** Continuing conflict without resolution between the parents over visitation and other issues concerning the child.
4. **Frequent Moves:** Lack of stability for the child at school and in friendships adds to insecurity and vulnerability.
5. **Harsh Punishment:** Harsh punishment and the absence of positive reinforcement and encouragement.
6. **Lack of Monitoring by Adults:** Children cannot be left to their own devices. Parents who abuse alcohol or drugs are putting themselves at high risk of being unable to monitor

their children effectively. Parents who are overextended, severely depressed, or too involved in their own concerns may be unable to be responsive, supportive, and interested in their child's day-to-day management.

7. **Aggressive Behavior:** Serious aggressive behavior, especially when it starts early and occurs in several settings—at home, in the neighborhood, or at school—is a threatening indicator of serious and long-term problems for boys of divorce.

8. **School Problems:** Poor school performance combined with lack of parental involvement with the school.

9. **Dangerous Neighborhood:** A dangerous neighborhood is a high-risk factor for children, especially when the child does not have meaningful relationships with children who are well adjusted. Access to guns, alcohol, and drugs, and relationships with children who are poorly monitored greatly increase risk.

All of these factors increase the odds against a child doing well.

Positive Outcomes

Lets review the positive outcomes of some of the boys we intrerviewed throughout this book.

Michael

We introduced Michael in Chapter 1 as the boy who was innocently asked by his pediatrician, "Who lives at home with you?" Michael had answered that he lived with his mother and father when in fact he was living with his grandparents while his biological mother was sorting out problems and deciding what to do about her son.

Let's review the starting point for Michael. His biological parents were in their late teenage years when Michael was conceived. They had started dating but in no way had developed a committed and long-term relationship. They expressed affection to each other and became sexually active. They did not recognize—or acknowledge—that their sexual activity, which seemed perfectly normal, would bring them across a threshold and into harm's way. They saw no danger in their activity, and their own parents were not aware of their sexual activity. Michael's mother became pregnant and for a while kept silent about her pregnancy. She did not seek prenatal care during her first trimester, and prior to the birth of the child the young woman married the "boyfriend" who got her pregnant. Neither teen was ready for successful employment, nor did they have a stable relationship. The marriage fell apart early and Michael's mother was left with primary care for her son. Michael's father had a few visits with his son soon after the divorce but quickly lost interest and withdrew.

For over two years Michael's mother had a difficult struggle that came to a climax when a new "lover" and companion "injured" her son. The physical abuse of Michael brought a difficult parenting situation to one of overwhelming crisis for the mother—and Michael.

The "adoption" of Michael did not come with one firm decision. At first Michael's mother brought her son over to her parents for them to take care of him "for a while." It was to be a temporary placement, Michael's mother would come back to bring Michael home with her. The "plan" became an illusion. Gradually, Michael's mother showed up at her parents place less and less often.

When Michael was three and a half his mother came to pick him up for a visit, and after a very short time, he asked to go back to his "mother and father"—clearly indicating his grandparents, with whom he had established a strong relationship, and they with him. During this time Michael's mother never did get back on track in terms of education, job training, or stable housing in a safe neighborhood.

By the time Michael turned six the arrangement had become permanent: Michael had been "adopted" by his grandparents. He went through his youth as a well-adjusted boy. He was a good student and developed a strong interest in sports. He was an able contributor—through effort and practice—in sandlot baseball and football. Michael had natural talent in artistic activities and the opportunity to develop skills during his childhood. He graduated from high school and college, is now married with two children, and owns and operates a successful small business.

When we talked to him recently, he reflected on his childhood. He expressed great appreciation for his grandparents for raising him and emphasized that they never gave the impression that he was an imposition on them. They never even gave a hint that they had to apologize or explain why they were raising him, but fully accepted him as their son. In addition, his grandparents spoke well of their daughter (Michael's mother) and showed him pictures of her when she was growing up. Michael said that his grandparents expressed sorrow over their daughter, and disappointment that she broke off contact with the family. This feeling of sorrow is understandable and essential. Given the circumstances, Michael appreciates his adoption by his grandparents.

The Option of Adoption

Michael grew up to be an outstanding person because he was rescued from a terribly troubled start with biological parents who were not equipped to raise him. He was adopted by parents who had a stable relationship and did their best to give him opportunities to develop his skills and interests. We strongly recommend adoption of children whose parents cannot or will not raise them effectively. It is the most viable option for children who face *all* of the following circumstances:

- The parents did not have a stable and committed relationship prior to the conception of their child.
- The father is not committed to parent and financially support the child.
- The mother does not have the education or job skills to help her raise the child in a minimumly adequate environment after she has received substantial help and intervention.

Parents Who Divorce but Remain Committed

John's Story

Remember John? His story began our book. He and his sister were told at a family picnic that his parents were going to divorce. At the time he felt shattered. He was also told that he would live with his mother and that his father would remain a father in every sense of the word. The rest of his story is one of hope, and we want to share it with you.

When his parents decided to divorce, a number of things happened. They agreed on an equitable financial settlement based on an accurate and unbiased appraisal of their worth. Their house was appraised and the value was included in the final settlement. Every financial consideration was discussed regarding the children, including their college education. John and his sister would be financially supported by their parents through their college years. We spoke recently with John's father, who said he is proud of his son's academic achievements and is pleased he has been accepted at a state university. John's father is willing to pay for his son's college education with pride.

John's father also said that when he and his wife decided to divorce they both expressed a commitment that their two children would not suffer because of the breakup. As we have seen,

John was greatly upset by the divorce, but he was able to go on with his life and develop emotionally.

We'll review some of the things that the parents did for John and his sister that served as protective factors to minimize some of the problems that can develop after a divorce:

- John was not raised without a father. His father kept a liberal visitation schedule, including annual two-week vacation with the children.
- John's father was concerned about all aspects of his children's lives and did not fall into the trap of occasional visits to a restaurant, with no involvement in his children's school success or other activities. Both parents maintained contact with the school, monitored their children's progress, and supported and encouraged them. Both parents kept up with their children's health and shared taking them for doctor and dentist appointments.
- Both parents cooperated on discipline and provided consistent rules, letting the children know they could not play one parent against the other.
- Both parents provided strict and consistent guidelines for their children's behavior and supervised them.
- Both parents clearly expressed their view that they were opposed to their children smoking or using alcohol or drugs.
- When the children became adolescents the parents set clear guidelines on behavior outside the home. The parents stayed informed as to their children's friends and companions and set limits on attending parties when no adult was available or willing to supervise.
- As John and his sister reached adolescence, both parents, by example and discussion, continued to provide information that would help their children develop a workable set of personal values.
- Both parents knew that in adolescence their children would

strive for independence—including independence from strict parental monitoring. They knew that the best way to accomplish this would be for the children to learn successful skills and attitudes.

- John's parents did not stop tracking his school efforts or his work habits. This required them to recognize a delicate balance between a growing child's need to be independent and their need as parents to focus responsibly on core issues.
- The mother was fortunate to remain in her neighborhood and maintain connections with friends and relatives. This provided important stability for her children, including John, who maintained close friendships all through his growing-up years.
- John's mother was connected to her community. She served on committees in her neighborhood and was active in church activities, which provided an important message to her children that being a part of a community is essential to being a citizen.

Carrilyn's Story

Although not an easy one, Carrilyn's story is also a success. Carrilyn divorced her husband of sixteen years after his third affair. Within months of the separation she found herself and her children slipping out of their comfortable upper-middle-class life and into poverty. At times her husband would "forget" to pay child support. At one point she was down to $14.75 in her checking account. Carrilyn had to apply for food stamps and found herself going to court to collect back support.

Much to her credit, Carrilyn never criticized her husband in front of the children. She felt it was important for them to have a good relationship with their father, and she never told her friends what Bill was doing to her and her family. Only her best friend and parents knew what was really happening.

During the divorce there was a time when Carrilyn and Bill's relationship became so bad they were no longer on speaking terms. Carrilyn would pass notes about the children to Bill in a notebook the kids took with them when they went to their father's house. She was determined that the children's welfare would always come first.

Then Bill "skipped" his weekends with the kids when a new woman entered his life. While Carrilyn did make Bill tell the children of his "change in plans" himself, she found herself in the awkward position of having to work to keep them interested in even seeing their father. And Bill's new focus came at a time when Carrilyn, after returning to college for a degree in X-ray technology really could have used some free time to study. Bill's help would have made her life a little easier.

At a time when Bill gave her every reason to be bitter and every opportunity to turn the children against him, she didn't. Instead she thought of what would be best for them in the long run—a good relationship with their father, even if he was behaving like a jerk. She would tell her best friend, "They have eyes. I don't have to tell the children any of their father's faults."

Thanks to their mother, Carrilyn's children did well despite hard times. Her son is on a scholarship at a prestigious East Coast university and her daughter is also on scholarship closer to home. Both children are well-adjusted and happy. Her son is grateful he was able to maintain a relationship with his father but he admires, respects, and values his mother. Both children have friends and seem unscarred by the trauma that their mother so carefully sheltered them from.

Carrilyn had to go the extra mile. She had to do much more than John's mother:

- She kept all relationships with her former spouse nonviolent.

- She persued legal ways of getting financial support from him, but did not keep the children from him even when he did not make his support payments.
- She made use of the financial help available to her (food stamps and Pell Grants—financial aid for education).
- She went back to school so she could support herself and her children as protection against Bill's unreliable financial support.
- She maintained communication with Bill concerning the children even through the worst of times.

Eventually, Carrilyn and Bill's relationship leveled off and they finally knew what to expect from each other. Bill finally stopped trying to get even with her by withholding child support, and Carrilyn, while always pleasant, had the court collect child support.

Children in single-parent homes can and do turn out well, and the steps these parents painfully took played a big part in helping the children adjust. Hopefully, you can see how the steps taken by Michael's relatives, John's family, and Carrilyn worked well for all the children.

10

Survival Techniques

Being a single mother is never easy, even under the best of circumstances. Single mothers always suffer from too many jobs, too little time to do them, and emotional and financial deprivation. In this book we have made an effort to help mothers see solutions to problems facing them. Now we would like to cover some survival skills. We're not talking green beret survival, just day-to-day survival, although there are probably days when you feel like you deserve combat pay for having made it through another really long day. What can a mother do to nurture herself as well as her son and other children?

Organize

In Chapter 3 we talked about ways to structure your life. Go over that chapter carefully from time-to-time for hints on time-saving techniques. Being organized is probably one of the best things you can do for yourself. Your time is very precious and very limited, so take a little time to organize and save a lot of wasted time later. One fairly organized mother we know asks for "organizers" for birthday and holiday gifts. She has gotten a pocket organizer (a purse calendar to organize and write down all of her tasks for the day), closet organizers, file cabinets, laundry room organizers, and even makeup organizers. Admittedly, these are not romantic gifts you can cherish, but you can cherish the time these practical gifts free up.

A Good Book, a Good Movie, a Good Friend

When you do have a free moment, make the most of it. Nurture your mind and soul. Read a book or go to a movie, preferably with a friend (that way you can do two things at once), or just visit someone you can talk to. There is something really comforting about spending time with an old and close friend: They accept you as you are, you don't have to explain your circumstances, your feelings, or even a bad mood. If your friend is another single mother, you can commiserate.

Do Tasks With a Friend

One mother we interviewed told us she and a friend helped each other clean their houses once a week. They were both going through divorces and could hardly get everything done alone, so every Saturday they got together and helped each other, cleaning one house in the morning the other in the afternoon. This gave them time to talk, share ideas, problems, and solutions. It also made doing housework much more fun, and again, they were able to do two things at once—an ideal situation.

You may be thinking, "I wouldn't want someone else to come in and help me clean." Maybe not, but the idea applies to many more situations. Go with a friend to the Laundromat, the grocery store, or meet once a month and cook freezer dinners together. Make enough spaghetti sauce for four or five dinners and freeze them. Prepare dinners that feed lots of people, divide them and freeze them. You and your friend will both be happy, and you'll have a quick, simple dinner when you come home and are in a rush.

Have a Good Laugh

Life is so much more bearable when you see the humor in it. There is nothing funny about being poor or lonely, but you will survive those situations if you try to find the humor in life's everyday mishaps.

One mother really had nothing to laugh about when she almost saw tragedy strike her father. Having her father live with her and her son had been wonderful for them. Ever since her husband had died her dad had made her life, as well as her son's, much happier. So you can imagine her concern when she thought her father was having a heart attack from years of smoking.

As she walked him into the emergency room they passed a cigarette machine. Her father, who could barely walk grasped his chest and pleaded, "Oh, please Mary, get me a cigarette."

She looked at him, unable to walk and hardly able to breathe, and said, "Dad, are you crazy? You're having a heart attack, I can't get you a cigarette."

Her father shot back, "But you don't understand. No matter how I look at this, it will probably be my last one."

For Mary, that was not a funny situation at the time, but weeks later, when her father was recovering from bypass surgery, and trying to talk every nurse with tobacco stains on her fingers out of a cigarette, she found the humor in it. Of course, it became funnier as she told it to family and friends.

Mary's ability to find humor in a tense situation helped her survive the stress of her father's illness. Finding humor in life is truly one of the best survival tips we have.

Prayer

Prayer and meditation are wonderful stress reducers. No matter what your faith or religious preference, prayer and meditation are very relaxing.

Prayer is both calming and powerful. It calms the soul while filling the spirit with power and energy. Prayer gives us a perspective on the past and the future, for in God's vast universe our troubles are small and will pass, and we can overcome almost anything.

For years communities have been built around churches and synagogues, and there was good reason for that: People have always found strength and comfort in them. Churches and synagogues also offer a supportive community of friends and fellow worshipers who share a value system that can be helpful to any mother raising a child today.

Exercise

Exercise is one of the best and healthiest ways to reduce stress. Before you tell yourself, "but I don't have time," make it. To be a good mother you have to *be* here. One of our single mothers gets up at six each morning to jog. It is the only free time she has, and she says it is one of the best things she does for herself. However, you don't have to be a jogger. You can swim, walk, or ride a bike.

Exercise not only increases your longevity, it gives you energy and makes you healthier *now*, so it holds long-term and short-term benefits. It reduces blood pressure and cholesterol while helping you control your weight, and it gives you the stamina you need for those twenty-six-hour days. An added benefit is improved health and fewer doctor bills. And if you exercise with friends, you are more likely to stick to it. Like everything else, exercise is more fun if you do it with a friend.

Learn to Talk to Yourself

Sometimes you have to be your own cheering section in the game of life. That's okay. When things look hopeless, give yourself a pep talk. Tell yourself, "I CAN do this. I can get through this test. I can feed a family of three on twenty dollars a week. I can do twenty-five hours of work in eighteen hours. I can go to work, to school, take care of two children and an apartment." One mother added, "And I can get a job as a magician."

In all seriousness, these little pep talks you give yourself are called affirmations, and they do help. Affirmations also work with children. Tell your son, "You will survive. You will do well on your math quiz. You will have a good soccer game. I know you will." Affirmations give us confidence and cheer us on. For your son they are also a reaffirmation of his mother's love and belief in him.

TLC

Mother yourself as well as your son. Be good to yourself. Take good care of yourself by exercising and eating a healthy diet with lots of fruits and vegetables. Go easy on the red meats and junk foods. Not only are they bad for you, they are expensive too.

Treat yourself to inexpensive luxury items like a hot bath, a cup of hot chocolate, or a library book. When you have a break in school or a day off from work, save an hour or two for yourself after the kids are in bed. Watch a movie on TV or do something you've wanted to do for ages but haven't had time for—that crossword puzzle or something fun. Try to remember to be as kind to yourself as you are to others.

Take a Class

Parenting classes are a wonderful way to do two things at once. You'll learn skills that will improve your relationship with your son, and you'll meet other parents.

You may feel you don't need a parenting class, but everyone who teaches them will tell you their class list always includes a number of teachers, counselors, and other professionals you would think had all the answers. A first-grade teacher confided:

"I'm almost embarrassed to be in here. But my son is thirteen, and I only specialize in K to three."

All parents of teenagers feel as though they could use some help. Parenting gives us new problems every day, and no one has all the answers. It is a difficult time for everyone, but a class makes it a little easier, especially when you know you're not the only one with these problems.

Getting Help If You Need It

If you need more than a class can offer, get help. As we said in the beginning of this chapter, being a single parent isn't easy; it is a long and lonely road to travel. If you can, take advantage of help that is available. We all need someone to talk to, and if you need the help of a counselor, get it. The appendix will give you the names and numbers of some national mentoring groups. In the chapter on improving your financial picture we offered lots of ideas on where you can go if you need emotional support or financial help. The important thing is to get help if you need it.

If counseling is available, take advantage of it. Most professionals know and understand how difficult it is for a single mother to raise children alone, and most are aware of the kind of help many mothers need. Remember, if this were a problem unique to you there wouldn't be so many programs and agencies set up to help women in the same situation. The fact is, most women in similar circumstances face very similar problems.

If you need to talk to someone and counseling is not available, think about a support group for single mothers. Many towns have Parents Without Partners groups. You may have one in your town or even a single parents' group in your church or synagogue. Never be afraid to make phone calls and ask questions. Other mothers who are going through what you are experiencing can be enormously helpful. A big part of surviving is getting help if you need it.

Take One Day at a Time: It Can Turn Out Well

While it is important to have long-range and short-range goals, you may want to take one day at a time so you can focus on little tasks that can be achieved. Some of the solutions we suggested, like college, can be overwhelming, but even big tasks are easily achieved when tackled one day at a time. You *can* turn your life around. Life can become overwhelming, but if you take it day-by-day, you *can* survive.

We have shared our stories with you in the hopes that you will see that even very difficult situations can turn out well. Raising a son without a father is not easy, but it can be done and done well. We hope our ideas make life a little easier for you and your son.

Where to Find Help

For Special Help

ACES (Association for Children for E)
2260 Upton Avenue
Toledo, OH 43606
(419) 472-6609

A group that helps parents collect child support. Offers information and emotional support to parents trying to collect child support.

Promise Keepers
P.O. Box 18376
Boulder, CO 80308

A mentor group for fathers. Helps men, even men separated from their children, be better fathers. This group is for men and does not always offer women equal support.

Mentoring Programs

California

Breakthrough Foundation: Youth at Risk
1952 Lombard Street
San Francisco, CA 94123
(415) 673-0171

A short-term mentoring program for children between the ages of 13 and 21. There is both mentoring and a wilderness course where children are taught to follow rules, take responsibilities, and be responsible to others in the group as well as rely on the group.

Asian-American Journalists Association (AAJA)
1765 Sutter Street, Suite 1000
San Francisco, CA 94115
(415) 346-2051

With thirteen chapters across the country, this group mentors Asian-Americans interested in journalism. It pairs experienced journalists with students in high school or college in entry-level jobs.

Connecticut

Association of School/Business Partnership Directors (ASBPD)
c/o Norwalk Public School
125 East Avenue
P.O. Box 6001
Norwalk, CT 06852
(203) 854-4011; fax: (203) 838-3299

Offers mentoring programs on a local basis and partnership programs with various school districts. (Formerly the National Alliance of Business/Education Partnerships.)

Colorado

Education Commission of the States (ECS)
707 17th Street, Suite 2700
Denver, CO 80202
(303) 299-3692

Offers a mentoring program with emphasis on academics and helping youths succeed.

Partner's Program, Inc.
165 Larimer Street, #730
Denver, CO 80202
(303) 595-4400

A one-on-one mentoring program that helps at-risk youths. Offers an extensive support system. Many groups in a number of states.

Georgia

Go to High School, Go to College
Atlanta, GA
(404) 766-5744

An academic mentoring program aimed at 11 to 21-year-old African-American males. Short- and long-term programs.

Project RAP (Reaching Adulthood Prepared)
Timothy Baptist Church
481 Timothy Road
Athens, GA 30606
(404) 549-1435

A mentoring program aimed at African-American males from 12 to 17 years of age.

YES! ATLANTA
955 Spring Street
Atlanta, GA 30309
(404) 874-6996

Aimed at 13 to 18-year-olds, this program offers both focused academic tutoring and job skills training as well as fundamental mentoring for children from the Projects.

Illinois

Project Image
765 E. 69th Place
Chicago, IL 60637
(312) 324-8700

Started and run by the black community churches, this mentoring program is aimed at African-American males from 8 to 18.

Project PEACE
534 E. 37th Street, 1st Floor
Chicago, IL 60653

A mentoring program that also stresses peer leadership, rites of passage, and life training skills. Aimed at children in the projects and schools from elementary to high school. Although the program emphasis changes slightly with each age group, all children have access to grief counseling for loss of a loved one through violence.

Young Men's Project
3030 W. Harrison Street
Chicago, IL 60612

6000 S. Wentworth Avenue
Chicago, IL 60621

Aimed at young African-American men from elementary to high school, this mentoring program also does academics.

Indiana

Kiwanis International
3636 Woodview Trace
Indianapolis, IN 46268
(317) 875-8755

Mentoring program that works with youth on social skills and vocational skills as wells as mentoring. Over 443 mentoring projects across the country.

Maryland

Project RAISE
605 N. Eutaw Street
Baltimore, MD 21201
(410) 685-8316

A mentoring program for at-risk youths from fifth to eighth grades.

Project 2000
Center for Educating African-American Males
Morgan State University
School of Education in Urban Studies

3083 Jenkins Hall
Baltimore, MD 21239
(410) 319-3275

A mentoring program for elementary-age males from female-headed, single-parent families.

Enterprise Foundation
505 American City Building
Columbia, MD 31044
(301) 964-1918

Mentoring programs in over thirty cities. Works with youths at-risk and their families. Job skills and counseling, adult literacy, and other support services.

Hands-on Science Outreach, Inc.
4910 Macon Road
Rockville, MD 20852
(301) 881-1142; fax: (301) 816-6934

For children from 4 to 12 years of age, this mentoring program encourages children in science with out of school science programs like after-school and summer programs.

National Association for the Advancement of Colored People (NAACP)
Back-to-School/Stay-in-School Program
4805 Mount Hope Drive
Baltimore, MD 21215
(301) 486-9149; 764-7357

Mentoring and tutoring program for children at risk of dropping out of school. Works on self-esteem and rewards school attendance and academic achievement.

Massachusetts

Center for Corporate and Education Initiatives
Brandeis University
Heller Graduate School
60 Turner Street
Waltham, MA 02254
(617) 736-4990

Mentoring program to help at-risk youths, underachievers and low-income students with skill building to help them get more education. Mentors help and support low income students through high school and college or technical school.

National Association of Independent Schools (NAIS)
74 Federal Street
Boston, MA 02110
(617) 451-2444; fax: (617) 482-3913

Mentoring and tutoring program featuring academic enrichment.

Partners for Disabled Youth
c/o Office of Handicapped Affairs
One Ashburton Place, Room 1305
Boston, MA 02108
(617) 727-7440; voice/TDD: (800) 322-2020

One-on-one mentoring program for disabled youths to develop potential talent and self-esteem with a positive role model.

Michigan

The Mentoring Association
Western Michigan University
A-121 Ellsworth Hall
Kalamazoo, MI 49008
(616) 387-4174

Mentoring program that encourages mentoring among a wide variety of organizations and agencies, businesses, and industries.

Missouri

Camp Fire Boys and Girls
National Headquarters
4601 Madison Avenue
Kansas City, MO 64112
(816) 756-0258

Well-known youth organization does group mentoring but also one-on-one as well. Does skill building.

New Jersey

Princeton Center for Leadership Training (PCLT)
12 Vandeventer Avenue
Princeton, NJ 08542
(609) 497-4870; fax: (609) 497-4879

Works on a number of mentoring services, peer mentoring, Partners in Learning, college and community mentoring, and teacher training and development. While it helps children from Kindergarten through twelfth grade, emphasis is on sixth to twelfth graders.

New York

Safe Kids/Safe Neighborhoods
New York City Department of Health
125 Worth Street, Box 46
New York, NY 10013
(212) 566-6121, 566-8003

This mentoring program, for children of all ages, also does parent training, job training, peer leadership, and recreation. Mentoring is for children and their mothers. Also does conflict resolution and social skills.

The Association of Junior Leagues
660 1st Avenue
New York, NY 10016
(212) 481-7196

Offers mentoring programs through community outreach. Also has some mentoring programs for young and single mothers.

The Chain Reaction Program
c/o March of Dimes Birth Defects Foundation
1275 Mamaroneck Avenue
White Plains, NY 10605
(914) 997-4465

Uses peer mentoring programs, teaches leadership skills.

Children's Aid Society Project Live
105 E. 22nd Street
New York, NY 10010

(212) 949-4925

Academic tutoring and mentoring program, one-on-one mentoring.

Educational Resources Information Center (ERIC)
Clearinghouse on Urban Education
Columbia University
Teachers College, Box 40
New York, NY 10027
(212) 678-3433

A clearing house with information and education on mentoring.

Girls Incorporated
30 E. 33rd Street
New York, NY 10016
(212) 689-3700

Mentoring program for girls in nontraditional jobs in business or trade jobs, and women in science and technology programs. Has operation SMART (Science, Math, and Relevant Technology).

Girl Scouts of the USA
830 3rd Avenue
New York, NY 10022
(212) 940-7739

Group mentoring program. Works on self-esteem and confidence building through skills.

March of Dimes
1275 Mamaroneck Avenue
White Plains, NY 10605
(914) 428-7100

Mentoring program aimed at preventing teen pregnancy and the birth defects associated with lack of prenatal care.

National Urban League
500 E. 62nd Street
New York, NY 10021
(212) 310-9212

Mentoring and guidance for at-risk African-American youths and families. Mentoring and tutoring.

One Hundred Black Men
105 E. 22nd Street
New York, NY 10010
(212) 777-7070

One-on-one mentoring to provide young black men with a positive male role model.

YWCA of the USA
726 Broadway
New York, NY 10003
(212) 614-2700

Mentoring and tutoring for at-risk teens.

I Have a Dream Foundation
31 W. 34th Street, 6th Floor
New York, NY 10001
(212) 736-1852

Helps students with mentoring and scholarship money for college.

Oregon

Mentoring Works
P.O. Box 3004-530
Corvallis, OR 97339
(503) 753-4170

Long-term, one-on-one mentoring programs for at-risk youths and mothers. Support systems interconnected.

Pennsylvania

Big Brothers/Big Sisters of America
230 N. 13th Street
Philadelphia, PA 19107
(215) 567-7000

Well-known and long-established mentoring program offers well-trained mentors. One of the biggest mentoring programs, with groups in almost every state. Provides one-on-one mentoring for at-risk youths.

Public/Private Ventures (P/PV)
399 Market Street
Philadelphia, PA 19106
(215) 592-9099; fax: (215) 592-0069

Works with the public and private sector to provide job skills, training, and employment opportunities for at-risk youths.

Uncommon Individual Foundation
3 Radnor Corporate Center
100 Matsonford Road, Suite 400
Radnor, PA 19087
(215) 964-3511; fax: (215) 527-0170

Trains mentors and does educational work. Keeps a data base and does research and publications.

Rhode Island

Campus Partners in Leaning (CPIL)—**Campus Compact**
c/o Campus Compact
Brown University
Box 1975
Providence, RI 02912
(401) 863-1119; fax: (401) 863-3779

College students mentoring at-risk youths in the community.

South Carolina

The National Dropout Prevention Center
Clemson University
Clemson, SC 29634
(803) 656-2599; fax: (803) 656-0136

Has a national data base with information on dropout prevention programs in the United States, speakers and organizations involved with dropout prevention. Also a mentoring program for at-risk youths and a mentoring guidebook.

Texas

Boy Scouts of America (BSA)
1325 Walnut Hill Lane
Irving, TX 75015
(214) 580-2000

Nationally-known group mentoring. Teaches skills and values.

Intercultural Development Research Association
5835 Callaghan Road, Suite 350
San Antonio, TX 78228
(512) 684-8180

Mentoring and tutoring program for at-risk students in middle schools in five cities.

Virginia

Cities in Schools, Inc. (CIS)
401 Wythe Street, Suite 200
Alexandria, VA 22314
(703) 519-8999

Mentoring, counseling, and employment counseling in schools.

National Association of Black Journalists (NABJ)
11600 Sunrise Valley Drive
Reston, VA 22091
(703) 648-1270

Sponsors a mentoring program in high schools and colleges for students interested in journalism. Also has scholarship and internship opportunities.

National Association of Partners in Education (NAPE)
209 Madison Street, Suite 200
Alexandria, VA 22314
(703) 836-4880

Emphasis on education and tutoring with mentoring component.

The National Volunteer Center
1111 N. 19th Street, Suite 500
Arlington, VA 22209
(703) 276-0542

Training and developing volunteer programs.

United Way of America
701 N. Fairfax Street
Alexandria, VA 22314
(703) 836-7112, ext. 419

Community outreach programs help at-risk youths with One-on-One
Partnership program. Mentors children and families.

Washington

Help One Student to Succeed (HOSTS)
1801 D Street, Suite 2
Vancouver, WA 98663
(206) 694-1705

Mentoring and tutoring to improve academic achievement. Program
can be purchased by school districts for kindergarten to twelfth-
grade use in schools.

Wisconsin

Family Service America
Department PM, Public Inquiry Specialist
11700 W. Lake Park Drive
Milwaukee, WI 53224
(414) 359-1040; fax: (414) 359-1079

Mentoring of single mothers and at-risk youths.

Washington D.C.

The Aspira Association, Inc.
1112 16th Street, N.W., Suite 340
Washington, DC 20036
(202) 835-3600

A mentoring program for Latin-American youths. Traditional and
group mentoring as well as academic tutoring. Teaches leadership
skills as well.

Black Male Youth Project
1510 9th Street, N.W.
Washington, DC 20077
(203) 332-0213

A mentoring program for males from 11 to 17 years old.

Delta Sigma Theta Sorority, Inc.
1707 New Hampshire Avenue, N.W.
Washington, DC 20009
(202) 483-5460

Largest black women's organization in the country. Mentors and tutors at-risk youths.

4-H Youth Development
Extension Service
U.S. Department of Agriculture
14 Street and Independence Avenue, N.W.
Room 3860-S Building
Washington, DC 20250
(202) 447-5332

Group mentoring and mentoring in drug education, teen pregnancy prevention, and mentoring programs for the handicapped. Strong mentoring component.

National Black Child Development Institute (NBCDI)
1462 Rhode Island Avenue, N.W.
Washington, DC 20005
(202) 387-1281

Mentoring and tutoring for African-American children to improve academic and job skills and self-esteem.

National Collaboration for Youth
1319 F Street, N.W., Suite 601
Washington, DC 20004
(202) 347-2080

Brings mentoring groups together.

National Council of La Raza (NCLR)
810 1st Street, N.E., Suite 300
Washington, DC 20002
(202) 289-8173

Hispanic-American mentoring group works on academic and job skills. In thirty-five states across the country.

National Education Association (NEA)
1201 16th Street, N.W.
Washington, DC 20036
(202) 822-7200

Individual members mentor at-risk youths in community partnership programs.

National Press Foundation
1282 National Press Building
Washington, DC 20045
(202) 662-7350

Helps promising minority students interested in journalism by pairing them with a minority journalist.

One-to-One
2801 M Street
Washington, DC 20007
(202) 338-3844; fax: (202) 338-1642

Mentoring program operated under the United Way.

Canada

The Mentoring Institute, Inc.
International Centre for Mentoring
675 Inglewood Avenue
West Vancouver, B.C., Canada V6E 2S9
(604) 684-4134; fax: (604) 925-1162

Peer Counseling

School Initiatives Program
149 9th Street
San Francisco, CA 94103
(415) 552-1250

Teens on Target
314 E. 10th Street
Oakland, CA 94606
(510) 635-8600, ext. 415

New Way of Fighting
878 Peachtree Street, N.E., Room 212
Atlanta, GA 30309
(404) 894-6617

Hawaii Mediation Program
University of Hawaii at Manoa
West Hall Annex 2, Room 222
1776 University Avenue,
Honolulu, HI 96822

RAPP (Resolve All Problems Peacefully)
Ferguson Middle School
701 January Avenue
Ferguson, MO 63135
(314) 521-5792

Project Reach
1 Orchard Street, 2nd Floor
New York, NY 10002
(212) 966-4227

Resolving Conflict Creatively Program
New York City Public Schools
163 3rd Avenue, #239
New York, NY 10003
(212) 260-6290

Violence Intervention Program (VIP)
Durham City Schools
Durham, NC 27702
(919) 966-5980

Parenting

California

Community Youth Gang Services Project
144 S. Fetterly Avenue
Los Angeles, CA 90022
(213) 266-4264

Crisis intervention and mediation; also: job counseling, environmental barriers, and recreational opportunities.

Richstone Family Center
13620 Cordary Avenue
Hawthorne, CA 90250
(213) 970-1921

Parenting classes; also: counseling and referral services.

Minnesota

Project STEEP (Steps Toward Effective, Enjoyable Parenting)
N548 Elliott Hall
75 E. River Road
Minneapolis, MN 55455
(612) 624-0210

Parenting classes, individual therapeutic intervention, and case management.

Missouri

Parents as Teachers
University of Missouri, Marinas Hall
8001 Natural Bridge Road
Street Louis, MO 63121
(314) 553-5738

Home visitation and group meetings by parent educators who teach parenting skills; screens for developmental problems and links with other services.

New York

Prenatal/Infancy Project
Elmira, NY
(716) 275-3738

Home visitation to teach parenting skills and basic health education.

Safe Kids/Safe Neighborhoods
New York City Department of Health
125 Worth Street, Box 46
New York, NY 10013
(212) 566-6121; 566-8003

Conflict resolution; also: social skills, parent training and support, mentoring, job training, peer leadership training, and recreation.

Ohio

Planned Futures
Brand Whitlock Community Center
642 Division Street
Toledo, OH 43602
(419) 698-2646

Parent program; also: family life education, job club, educational help, education on history and culture, sports, and physical and mental health services.

PATHS: Promoting Adolescents Through Health Service
Children's Hospital Medical Center of Akron
377 S. Portage Path
Akron, OH 44320
(216) 535-7000

Parent education; also: family life and sex education, health care, counseling, fitness activities, theater and dance, tutoring, and career awareness program.

Therapeutic Activities

California

Community Youth Gang Services
144 S. Fetterly Avenue
Los Angeles, CA 90022
(213) 266-4264

Recreational opportunities; also: crisis intervention and mediation, job counseling, environmental barriers.

Richstone Family Center
13620 Cordary Avenue
Hawthorne, CA 90250
(213) 970-1921

Counseling and referral; also: parenting classes.

Massachusetts

Good Grief Program
295 Longwood Avenue
Boston, MA 02115
(617) 232-8390

Crisis intervention consultation for teachers, administrators, parents.

Violence Prevention Project
Health Promotion Program for Urban Youth
1010 Massachusetts Avenue, 2nd Floor
Boston, MA 02118
(617) 534-5196

Identification of youths with high-risk behavior, counseling, public service announcements, educational media, and conflict resolution curriculum.

Michigan

Save Our Sons and Daughters (SOSAD)
453 Martin Luther King Boulevard
Detroit, MI 48201
(303) 833-3030

Family support of children who have been killed; also: public awareness campaigns, community marches, and lobbying for the elimination of handguns.

New Mexico

Santa Fe Mountain Center
Route 4, Box 34C
Sante Fe, NM 87501
(505) 983-6158

Counseling recreational opportunities; also: educational programs, conflict resolution, social skills, communication, and problem solving.

New York

Project Reach
1 Orchard Street, 2nd Floor
New York, NY 10002
(212) 966-4227

Individual and family crisis counseling, school and court advocacy; also: peer counseling and training.

Ohio

PATHS: Promoting Adolescents Through Health Service
Children's Hospital Medical Center of Akron
377 S. Portage Path
Akron, OH 44320
(216) 535-7000

Counseling; also: family life and sex education, health care, fitness activities, theater and dance, tutoring, career awareness program, and parent education.

Planned Futures
Brand Whitlock Community Center
642 Division Street
Toledo, OH 43602
(419) 698-2646

Counseling; also: Family life education, job club, educational help, education on history and culture, sports, physical health services, and parent program.

Pennsylvania

House of Umoja Boystown
1410 N. Frazier Street
Philadelphia, PA 19131
(215) 473-5893

Surrogate family, remedial basic education, vocational education and counseling, life skills training, conflict resolution, and recreation.

Philadelphia Injury Prevention Program
500 S. Broad Street
Philadelphia, PA 19146
(215) 875-5657

Crisis intervention, community education, and counseling victims to prevent retaliation.

The Violence Postvention Program
Philadelphia Injury Prevention Program
Philadelphia Department of Public Health
500 South Broad Street
Philadelphia, PA 19146
(215) 875-5657

Crisis intervention, group therapy, and peer and community relations.

Texas

Dallas Independent School District Crisis Management Plan
3700 Ross Avenue
Dallas, TX 75204
(214) 565-6700

Coordinated response to crises, counseling, and referral.

Virginia

Cities in Schools
401 Wythe Street, Suite 200
Alexandria, VA 22314
(703) 519-8999

Counseling, employment, recreation, and legal assistance services brought to school.

Washington, D.C.

Howard University Violence Prevention Project
Department of Psychology, Howard University
525 Bryant Street, N.W.
Washington, DC 20011
(202) 806-6805

Counseling, parent support, teacher training; also: conflict resolution, and development of social skills.

Recreational Activities

California

Challengers Boys Club
5029 S. Vermont Avenue
Los Angeles, CA 90037
(213) 971-6161

Recreational activities, also: social development and strict code of rules including restrictions against wearing gang-related clothing.

Community Youth Gang Services
144 S. Fetterly Avenue
Los Angeles, CA 90022
(213) 266-4264

Recreational opportunities; also: crisis intervention and mediation, job counseling, and environmental barriers.

Illinois

Chicago Commons Association
915 N. Wolcott
Chicago, IL 60622
(312) 342-5330

Recreational activities; also: case managment support, job training, and work opportunities.

Missouri

Urban Interpersonal Violence Injury Control Project
2360 E. Linwood
Kansas City, MO 64109
(816) 861-9100

Recreational and social opportunities; also: educational program on conflict resolution, anger control, and problem solving.

New Mexico

Santa Fe Mountain Center
Route 4, Box 34C
Santa Fe, NM 87501
(505) 983-6158

Recreational opportunities; also: educational programs, conflict resolution, social skills, communication, and problem solving.

Youth Development, Inc.
1710 Centro Familiar, S.W.
Albuquerque, NM 87105
(505) 873-1604

Recreational opportunities; also: educational activities and work opportunities.

New York

Safe Kids/Safe Neighborhoods
New York City Department of Health
125 Worth Street, Box 46
New York, NY 10013
(212) 566-6121; 566-8003

Recreation; also: social skills, parent training and support, mentoring, job training, peer leadership training, and recreation.

Ohio

PATHS: Promoting Adolescents Through Health Service
Children's Hospital Medical Center of Akron
377 S. Portage Path
Akron, OH 44320
(216) 535-7000

Expression through theater and dance, fitness activities; also: counseling.

Planned Futures
Brand Whitlock Community Center
642 Division Street
Toledo, OH 43602
(419) 698-2646

Sports; also: counseling, family life education, job club, educational help, education on history and culture, physical health services, and parent program.

Pennsylvania

House of Umoja Boystown
1410 N. Frazier Street
Philadelphia, PA 19131
(215) 473-5893

Surrogate family, remedial basic education, vocational education and counseling, life skills training; also: conflict resolution training and recreation.

South Carolina

Midnight Hoops Program
Columbia, SC
(803) 777-5709

Recreation

Virginia

Cities in Schools
401 Wythe Street, Suite 200
Alexandria, VA 22314
(703) 519-8999

Counseling, employment, recreation, and legal assistance services brought to schools.

Conflict Resolution

California

School Initiatives Program
149 9th Street
San Francisco, CA 94103
(415) 552-1250

Conflict resolution training; also: peer conflict managers.

Illinois

Voyageur Outward Bound School
500 W. Madison Street, Suite 2100
Chicago, IL 60606
(312) 715-0550

Conflict resolution training;, also: wilderness and urban adventure course that teaches group cooperation, communication, and alternatives to violent solutions.

Massachusetts

Violence Prevention Project
Health Promotion Program for Urban Youth
1010 Massachusetts Avenue, 2nd Floor
Boston, MA 02118
(617) 534-5196

Conflict resolution curriculum; also: public service announcements, educational media, identification of high-risk youths, counseling.

Missouri

Urban Interpersonal Violence Injury Control Project
2360 E. Linwood
Kansas City, MO 64109
(818) 861-9100

Educational program on conflict resolution and anger control; also: problem solving, recreational and social opportunities.

New Mexico

Santa Fe Mountain Center
Route 4, Box 34C
Santa Fe, NM 87501
(505) 983-6158

Educational programs, social skills, communication, and problem solving; also: conflict resolution, counseling, and recreational opportunities.

New York

Resolving Conflict Creatively Program
163 3rd Avenue, #239
New York, NY 10003
(212) 260-6290

Conflict resolution curriculum; also: student mediation.

Safe Kids/Safe Neighborhoods
New York City Department of Health
125 Worth Street, Box 46
New York, NY 10013
(212) 566-6121; 566-8003

Conflict resolution; also: social skills, parent training and support, mentoring, job training, peer leadership training, and recreation.

North Carolina

Violence Intervention Program (VIP)
Durham City Schools
Durham, NC 27702
(919) 966-5980

Conflict resolution; also: teacher training and peer counselors
(eighth-grade students for sixth-grade students).

Violence Prevention Program
Mecklenburg County Health Department
249 Billingsley Road
Charlotte, NC 28211
(704) 336-6443

Conflict resolution, support groups.

The Youth Gang Drug Prevention Program
Mecklenburg County Health Department
249 Billingsley Road
Charlotte, NC 28211
(704) 336-6443

Conflict resolution; also: recreation.

Washington, D.C.

Washington Community Violence Prevention Program
Washington Hospital Center
Room 4B-46
110 Irving Street, N.W.
Washington, DC 20010
(202) 877-3761

Conflict resolution training, education about risk factors for violence,
and problem solving; also: public information media campaign.

Training in Life and Social Skills

Arizona

Chicanos por la Causa
1112 E. Buckeye Road
Phoenix, AZ 85034
(602) 257-0700

Education; also: counseling and job placement.

California

Breakthrough Foundation: Youth at Risk
1952 Lombard Street
San Francisco, CA 94123
(415) 673-0171

Wilderness course stressing rules, responsibility, and reliance on the group; also: mentoring.

Community Youth Gang Services Project
144 S. Fetterly Avenue
Los Angeles, CA 90022
(213) 266-4264

Crisis intervention and mediation; also: job counseling, environmental barriers, recreational opportunities.

Gang Prevention and Intervention Program
Turning Point Family Services, Inc.
1602 S. Brookhurst Street
Anaheim, CA 92804

Curriculum on self-esteem, decision-making skills, and other issues related to gangs.

HAWK Federation for Manhood Development and Training Program
175 Filbert Street, Suite 202
Oakland, CA 94607
(510) 836-3245

High school curriculum, cultural problem-solving skills, interpersonal skills, character development, and academic and decision-making skills.

102nd Street Elementary School
Los Angeles, CA 90003

Classes on grief and loss.

Southeast Community Day Center School
9525 E. Imperial Highway
Downey, CA 90242
(213) 922-6821

Classroom education and life skills training; also: job skills training and work opportunities.

The Paramount Plan: Alternatives to Gang Membership
16400 Colorado Avenue
Paramount, CA 90723
(213) 220-2140

Curriculum for students; also: parent/community awareness.

Connecticut

The New Haven Social Development Program
Department of Social Development
New Haven Public School System
James Hilihouse High School
New Haven, CT 06511
(203) 772-7443

Curriculum that helps students acquire socially competent behavior.

Illinois

African-American Male Education Network (AMEN)
9824 S. Western Avenue, Suite 175
Chicago, IL 60643
(708) 720-0235

Rites of passage, advocacy, and education for male and female responsibility and parenting.

Leadership Development Institute
2137 W. 54th Street
Chicago, IL 60609
(708) 868-8411

Rites of passage, cultural awareness, male and female responsibility, stress management, violence prevention, sex education, and parenting.

Metropolitan Area Child Study (MACS)
University of Illinois at Chicago
Department of Psychology (M/C 285)
Chicago, IL 60680
(312) 996-2600

Development of nonagressive norms for behavior, reduction of hostile bias, and encouragement of prosocial behavior.

Project PEACE
534 E. 37th Street, 1st Floor
Chicago, IL 60653
(312) 791-4768

Mentoring; also: peer leadership, peer mediation, rites of passage, grief counseling, and life training.

Viewpoints Training Program
University of Illinois at Chicago
Center for Research on Aggression
Department of Psychology (M/C 285)
P.O. Box 4348, Chicago, IL 60680
(312) 413-2624

Curriculum for group sessions that teach skills for solving social problems and alternatives to violent behavior.

Voyageur Outward Bound School
500 W. Madison Street, Suite 2100
Chicago, IL 60606
(312) 715-0550

Wilderness and urban adventure course that teaches group cooperation, communication, and alternatives to violent solutions; also: conflict resolution training.

Young Men's Project
3030 W. Harrison Street
Chicago, IL 60612

6000 S. Wentworth Avenue
Chicago, IL 60621

Curriculum development; also: mentoring.

Massachusetts

Barron Assessment and Counseling Center
25 Walk Hill Street
Jamaica Plain, MA 02130
(617) 635-8123

Education on violence prevention; also: individual and group counseling.

Boston Conflict Resolution Program
Boston Area Educators for Social Responsibility
11 Garden Street
Cambridge, MA 02138
(617) 492-8820

Teacher training programs, support groups, peer mediation, curricula on conflicts that commonly occur in school settings and ways to deal with conflict.

Good Grief Program
295 Longwood Avenue
Boston, MA 02115
(617) 232-8390

Crisis intervention, consultation for teachers, administrators, and parents.

Michigan

Southeastern Michigan Spinal Cord Injury System
261 Mack Avenue
Detroit, MI 48201
(313) 745-9740

Videotape program and discussion guide about gunshot victims.

Where Have All the Children Gone?
New Center Community Mental Health Services
2051 W. Grand Boulevard
Detroit, MI 48208
(313) 895-4000

Curriculum on awareness of violence and problem-solving skills.

Minnesota

Climb Theatre
500 N. Robert Street, Suite 220
St. Paul, MN 55101
(612) 227-9660

Violence education for children, including a play, curriculum, and psychological counseling (does a production called *Ouch*).

Missouri

Urban Interpersonal Violence Injury Control Project
2360 E. Linwood
Kansas City, MO 64109
(816) 861-9100

Educational program on conflict resolution and anger control; also: problem solving, recreational and social opportunities.

New Mexico

Santa Fe Mountain Center
Route 4, Box 34C
Santa Fe, NM 87501
(505) 983-6158

Conflict resolution; also: educational programs, social skills, communication, problem solving, counseling, and recreational opportunities.

Youth Development, Inc.
1710 Centro Familiar, S.W.
Albuquerque, NM 87105
(505) 873-1604

Educational activities; also: work and recreational opportunities.

New York

Children's Creative Response to Conflict
523 N. Broadway, Box 271
Nyack, NY 10960
(914) 358-4601

Classroom workshops that emphasize cooperation, communication, bias awareness; also: conflict resolution.

Early Adolescent Helper Program
25 W. 43rd Street, Room 620
New York, NY 10036
(212) 642-2307

Curriculum on human development; also: community involvement, learning job skills.

Safe Kids/Safe Neighborhoods
New York City Department of Health
125 Worth Street, Box 46
New York, NY 10013
(212) 566-6121; 566-8003

Job training; also: social skills, parent training and support, mentoring, recreation.

North Carolina

Male Health Alliance for Life Extension (MHALE)
10 Sunnybrook Road
P.O. Box 1409
Raleigh, NC 27620
(919) 250-4535

Life skills training; also: remedial basic education, vocational education and counseling, and conflict resolution.

Ohio

Planned Futures
Brand Whitlock Community Center
642 Division Street
Toledo, OH 43602
(419) 698-2646

Family life education; also: job club, educational help, education on history and culture, sports, physical and mental health services, and parent program.

PATHS: Promoting Adolescents Through Health Service
Children's Hospital Medical Center of Akron
377 S. Portage Path
Akron, OH 44320
(216) 535-7000

Family life and sex education; also: health care, counseling, fitness activities, theater and dance, tutoring, career awareness program, and parent education.

Pennsylvania

Philadelphia Injury Prevention Program
Philadelphia Health Department
500 S. Broad Street
Philadelphia, PA 19146
(215) 875-5661

Crisis intervention counseling victims to prevent retaliation; also: community education.

House of Umoja Boystown
1410 N. Frazier Street
Philadelphia, PA 19131
(215) 473-5893

Surrogate family, remedial basic education, vocational education and counseling, and life skills training; also: conflict resolution training and recreation.

Washington

PATHS: Providing Alternative Thinking Strategies
University of Washington
Seattle, WA 98195

Curriculum that stresses adaptive capabilities, self control, emotional understanding, and problem solving.

Washington, D.C.

Channeling Children's Anger
Institute for Mental Health Initiatives
4545 42nd Street, N.W., Suite 311
Washington, DC 20016
(202) 364-7111

Anger management curriculum.

Project SPIRIT
1225 Eye Street, N.W., Suite 750
Washington, DC 20005
(202) 371-1091

After-school curriculum, life skills training, pastoral counseling, training, and parenting education.

Teens, Crime, and the Community
National Crime Prevention Council
1700 K Street, N.W., Suite 200
Washington, DC 20006
(202) 466-6272

Curriculum on how students can reduce their chances of becoming a victim and encouraging students to participate in community projects.

Wisconsin

Milwaukee Public Schools
P.O. Drawer 10K
Milwaukee, WI 53201
(414) 475-8393

Immersion schools.

Work Opportunities

Arizona

Chicanos por la Causa
1112 E. Buckeye Road
Phoenix, AZ 85034
(602) 257-0700

Job placement; also: education and counseling.

California

Community Youth Gang Services
144 S. Fetterly Avenue
Los Angeles, CA 90022
(213) 266-4264

Job counseling; also: recreational opportunities, crisis intervention and mediation, and environmental barriers.

Southeast Community Day Center School
9525 East Imperial Highway
Downey, CA 90242
(213) 922-6821

Job skills training and work opportunities; also: classroom education and life skills training.

Illinois

Chicago Commons Association
915 N. Wolcott
Chicago, IL 60622
(312) 342-5330

Job training and work opportunities; also: recreational activities and case management support.

New Mexico

Youth Development, Inc.
1710 Centro Familiar, S.W.
Albuquerque, NM 87105
(505) 873-1604

Work opportunities; also: recreational opportunities and educational activities.

New York

Early Adolescent Helper Program
25 W. 43rd Street, Room 620
New York, NY 10036
(212) 642-2307

Community involvement and learning job skills; also: curriculum on human development.

Safe Kids/Safe Neighborhoods
New York City Department of Health
125 Worth Street, Box 46
New York, NY 10013
(212) 566-6121; 566-8003

Job training; also: social skills, parent training and support, mentoring, and recreation.

North Carolina

Male Health Alliance for Life Extension (MHALE)
10 Sunnybrook Road
P.O. Box 1409
Raleigh, NC 27620
(919) 250-4535

Vocational education and counseling; also: remedial education, vocational education and counseling, life skills training, and conflict resolution.

The Youth Gang Drug Prevention Program
Mecklenburg County Health Department
249 Billingsley Road
Charlotte, NC 28211
(704) 336-6443

Recreation and teen clubs; also: conflict resolution.

Ohio

Planned Futures
Brand Whitlock Community Center
642 Division Street
Toledo, OH 43602
(419) 698-2646

Job club; also: family life education, educational help, education on history and culture, sports, physical and mental health services, and parent program.

Virginia

Cities in Schools
401 Wythe Street, Suite 200
Alexandria, VA 22314
(703) 519-8999

Counseling, employment, recreation and legal assistance services brought to schools.

Peer Counseling

California

School Initiatives Program
149 9th Street
San Francisco, CA 94103
(415) 552-1250

Teens on Target
314 E. 10th Street
Oakland, CA 94606
(510) 635-8600, ext. 415

Georgia

New Way of Fighting
878 Peachtree Street, N.E., Room 212
Atlanta, GA 30309
(404) 894-6617

Hawaii

Hawaii Mediation Program
University of Hawaii at Manoa
West Hall Annex 2, Room 222
1776 University Avenue
Honolulu, HI 97822

Missouri

RAPP (Resolve All Problems Peacefully)
Ferguson Middle School
701 January Avenue
Ferguson, MO 63135
(314) 521-5792

New York

Project Reach
1 Orchard Street, 2nd Floor
New York, NY 10002
(212) 966-4227

Resolving Conflict Creatively Program
New York City Public Schools
163 3rd Avenue, #239
New York, NY 10003
(212) 260-6290

North Carolina

Violence Intervention Program (VIP)
Durham City Schools
Durham, NC 27702
(919) 966-5980

Notes

♦ ♦ ♦ ♦ ♦

Chapter 1

1. J. Wallerstein and S. Blakeslee, *Second Chances: Men, Women, and Children a Decade After Divorce,* (London: Grant McIntyre, 1990).

2. Ibid.

3. Annie E. Casey Foundation, "Kids Count," report, April 1995.

4. K. A. Crnic, "Mental Retardation," *Behavioral Assessment of Childhood Disorders,* 2nd ed., E. J. Mash and L. G. Terdal, eds., (New York: Guilford Press, 1988).

5. Annie E. Casey Foundation, op. cit.

6. U.S. Advisory Board on Child Abuse and Neglect, *Child Abuse and Neglect: Critical First Steps in Response to a National Emergency,* (Washington, D.C.: U.S. Government Printing Office, 1990.)

7. D. B. Downey, "The School Performance of Children From Single-Mother and Single-Father Families: Economic or Interpersonal Deprivation?" *Journal of Family Issues* 15, no. 1: 129–47 (March 1994).

8. A. P. Thomas, *Crime and the Sacking of America,* (Washington, D. C.: Brassey's Inc., 1994.

9. D. J. Hernandez, *America's Children: Resources for Families, Government and the Economy,* (New York: Russell Bage Foundation, 1993).

10. J. Ladd, *Out of the Madness,* (New York: Warner Books, 1994).

11. Ibid., p. 20.

12. Ibid., p. 22.

13. Megan Rosenfeld, "My Father's House Has Many Mansions," *Washington Post,* national weekly ed., Sept. 11–17, 1995.

Chapter 2

1. S. McLanahan and K. Booth, "Mother-Only Families: Problems, Prospects, and Politics," *Journal of Marriage and the Family* 51: 557–80 (1988).

2. Ibid.

3. J. D. Teachman and K. M. Paasch, "Financial Impact of Divorce on Children and Their Families," *The Future of Children: Children and Divorce*, Richard E. Behrman, ed. The David and Lucile Packard Foundation, 4, no. 1: 63–83 (1994).

4. J. R. Carbone, "A Feminist Perspective on Divorce," *The Future of Children: Children and Divorce*, Richard E. Behrman, ed., The David and Lucile Packard Foundation, 4, no. 1: 183–209 (1994).

5. Annie E. Casey Foundation, op. cit.

6. Robert B. Reich and Laura D'Andrea Tyson, "This is NO WAY TO REWARD WORK," *Washington Post*, national weekly ed., July 31–Aug. 6, 1995.

7. "Restore the Floor...It's Time to Raise the Minimum Wage," AFL–CIO report no. 86, October 1995.

8. Bureau of Labor Statistics. U.S. Department of Labor, Office of Productivity and Technology, "Country Reports on Human Rights Practices for 1994."

9. F. D. Blav and L. M. Kahn, "The Gender Earnings Gap: Some International Evidence," *Differences and Changes in Wage Structures*, Richard B. Freeman and Lawrence F. Katz, eds., (1995) 105–44.

10. AFL–CIO report no. 86, op. cit.

11. Blav and Kahn, op. cit.

12. Douglas J. Besharov, "Welfare Reform Without Illusions," *Washington Post*, national weekly ed., July 31–Aug. 6, 1995.

13. P. G. Roberts, "Problem Support Orders: Problem With Enforcement," *The Future of Children: Children and Divorce*, Richard E. Behrman, ed., The David and Lucile Packard Foundation, 4, no. 1: 183–209 (1994).

14. Teachman and Paasch, op. cit.

15. I. Garfinkel, M. S. Melli, and J. G. Robertson, "Child Support Orders: A Perspective on Reform," *The Future of Children: Children and Divorce*, Richard E. Behrman, ed., The David and Lucile Packard Foundation, 4, no. 2: 84–100 (1994).

16. R. Todd, *Collect Your Child Support*, (National Legal Services, 1994).

Chapter 4

1. J. Tallmadge and R. A. Barkley, "The Interactions of Hyperactive and Normal Boys With Their Mothers and Fathers," *Journal of Abnormal Child Psychology*, 11: 565–79 (1983).

2. American Association of Pediatrics, "Violence in the Home: Findings, Recommendations, and Action Steps," *Pediatrics* 94, no. 4: 579–86 (1994).

3. M. A. Straus, R. J. Gilles, and S. K. Steinmetz, *Behind Closed Doors: Violence in the American Family*, (Garden City, N.J.: Anchor Books, 1981).

4. L. S. Wissow and D. Roter, "Toward Effective Discussion of Discipline and Corporal Punishment During Primary Care Visits: Findings From Studies of Doctor-Patient Interaction," *Pediatrics* 94, no. 4: 587–93 (1994).

5. S. J. Holmes and L. N. Robins, "The Role of Parental Disciplinary Practices in the Development of Depression and Alcoholism," *Psychiatry* 51: 24–36 (1988).

Chapter 5

1. F. P. Rice, *Human Development: A Life-Span Approach*, 2nd ed., (Englewood Cliffs, N.J.: Prentice Hall, 1995).

2. S. F. Kerin and A. H. Beller, "Educational Attainment of Children From Single-Parent Families: Differences by Exposure, Gender, and Race," *Demography* 25: 221–24 (1988).

Chapter 6

1. I. Garfinkel and S. McLanahan, *Single Mothers and Their Children: A New American Dilemma*, (Washington, D.C.: The Urban Institute, 1986).

2. Ellen D. Bassuk, M.D., *Community Care for Homeless Families*, (Newton Center, Mass.: The Better Homes Foundation, 1990).

Chapter 7

1. G. B. Melton and F. D. Barry, "Neighbors Helping Neighbors: The Vision of the U.S. Advisory Board on Child Abuse and Neglect," *Protecting Children From Abuse and Neglect: Foundation for a New National Strategy*, G. B. Melton and F. D. Barry, eds., (New York: Guilford Press, 1994), 1–13.

2. D. A. Wolfe, "Child Abuse and Neglect," *Behavioral Assessment of Childhood Disorders*, 2nd ed., E. J. Mash and L. G. Terdal, eds. (New York: Guilford Press, 1988), 402–44.

3. D. A. Wolfe and A. McEachran, "Child Abuse and Neglect," *Behavioral Assessment of Childhood Disorders*, 3rd ed., E. J. Mash and L. G. Terdal, eds. (New York: Guilford Press, 1988).

4. Ibid.

5. D. Finkelhor and Russell, "Women as Perpetrators of Sexual Abuse: Review of the Evidence," *Child Sexual Abuse: New Theory and Research*, D. Finkelhor, ed., (New York: Free Press, 1984), 171–87.

6. G. Abel, et al., "Multiple Paraphilic Diagnoses Among Sex Offenders," *Bulletin of the American Academy of Psychiatry and the Law* 16, no. 2: 153–68 (1988).

7. V. V. Wolfe and D. A. Wolfe, "The Sexually Abused Child," *Behavioral Assessment of Childhood Disorders*, 2nd ed., E. J. Mash and L. G. Terdal, eds. (New York: Guilford Press, 1988), 670–714.

8. Ibid.

9. Ibid.

10. J. P. Foreyt and J. K. McGavin, "Anorexia Nervosa and Bulimia," *Behavioral Assessment of Childhood Disorders*, 2nd ed., E. J. Mash and L. G. Terdal, eds. (New York: Guilford Press, 1988), 776–805.

11. Ibid.

12. P. R. Amato, "Life-Span Adjustment of Children to Their Parents' Divorce," *The Future of Children: Children and Divorce*, R. E. Behrman, ed., The David and Lucile Packard Foundation, 143–64 (1994).

13. Angela Phillips, *In Trouble With Boys*, (New York: Basic Books, 1994).

14. Nathan McCall, *Makes Me Wanna Holler*, (New York: Random House, 1994).

15. Ibid.

Chapter 8

1. a) V. King, "Nonresident Father Involvement and Child Well-Being: Can Dads Make a Difference." *Journal of Family Issues* 15, 78–96, 1994.

b) Masako Ishii-Kruntz, "Paternal Involvement and Perception Toward Fathers' Roles: A Comparison Between Japan and the United States," *Journal of Family Issues* 15, 30–48, 1994.

2. Pat Ordovensky, "Both Sides Win With Mentoring," Lewis Harris Poll, *USA Today*, March 28, 1990.

Bibliography

◆ ◆ ◆ ◆ ◆

Abel, G., et al. "Multiple Paraphilic Diagnoses Among Sex Offenders." *Bulletin of the American Academy of Psychiatry and the Law* 16, no. 2 (1988): 153–68.

Amato, Paul R. "Father-Child Relations, Mother-Child Relations, and Offspring Psychological Well-Being in Early Adulthood." *Journal of Marriage and the Family* 56 (1994): 1031–42.

————. "Life-Span Adjustment of Children to Their Parents' Divorce," in *The Future of Children: Children and Divorce*, edited by R. H. Behrman, vol. 4, no. 1: 143–54. Los Altos, Calif.: The David and Lucile Packard Foundation, 1994.

American Association of Pediatrics, "Violence in the Home: Findings, Recommendations, and Action Steps." *Pediatrics* 94, no. 4 (1994): 579–86.

Annie E. Casey Foundation. "Kids Count" report. Baltimore: Annie E. Casey Foundation, April 1995.

Bassuk, Ellen L., et al. *Community Care for Homeless Families.* Newton Center, Mass.: Better Homes Foundation, 1990.

Besharov, Douglas J. "Welfare Reform Without Illusions." *The Washington Post National Weekly Edition*, July 31–August 6, 1995.

Blav, F. D., and L. M. Kahn. "The Gender Earnings Gap: Some International Evidence," in *Differences and Changes in Wage Structures*, edited by Richard B. Freeman and Lawrence F. Katz. Chicago: University of Chicago Press, 1995, 105–144.

Brewer, Rose M. "Black Women in Poverty: Some Comments on Female-Headed Families." *Journal of Women in Culture and Society* 13 (1988): 331–39.

Carbone, J. R. "A Feminist Perspective on Divorce," in *The Future of Children: Children and Divorce*, edited by R. E. Behrman, vol. 4, no. 1: 183–209. Los Altos, Calif. The David and Lucile Packard Foundation, 1994.

Centers for Disease Control. *The Prevention of Youth Violence.* Washington, D.C.: U.S. Department of Health and Human Services, 1993.

"Country Reports on Human Rights Practices for 1994." Bureau of Labor Statistics. Washington, D.C.: U.S. Department of Labor, Office of Productivity and Technology.

Crinic, K. A. "Mental Retardation," in *Behavioral Assessment of Childhood Disorders,* (2nd edition) edited by E. J. Mash and L. G. Terdal. New York: Guilford Press, 1988.

Downey, Douglas B. "The School Performance of Children From Single-Mother and Single-Father Families: Economic or Interpersonal Deprivation?" *Journal of Family Issues* 15, no. 1 (1994): 129–47.

Ferrara, Frank. *On Being Father.* Garden City, N.Y.: Doubleday, 1985.

Finkelhor, D. and Russell Finkelhor. "Women as Perpetrators of Sexual Abuse: Review of the Evidence," in *Child Sexual Abuse: New Theory and Research,* edited by D. Finkelhor. New York: Free Press, 1984, 171–87.

Foreyt, J. P., and J. K. McGavin. "Anorexia Nervosa and Bulimia," in *Behavioral Assessment of Childhood Disorders: Second Edition,* edited by E. J. Mash and L. G. Terdal. New York: Guilford Press, 1996, 776–805.

Furstenberg, Frank F., Jr. "Parenting Apart: Patterns of Childrearing After Marital Disruption." *Journal of Marriage and the Family* 47, no. 4 (November 1985): 893–904.

Garfinkel, I., et al. "Child Support Orders: A Perspective on Reform," in *The Future of Children: Children and Divorce,* edited by R. E. Behrman, vol. 4, no. 2: 84–100. Los Altos, Calif.: The David and Lucile Packard Foundation, 1994.

Garfinkel, I., and S. McLanahan. "Single Mothers and Their Children: A New American Dilemma." Washington, D.C.: The Urban Institute, 1992.

Hernandez, D. J. "Government and the Economy," in *America's Children: Resources for Families.* New York: Russell Sage Foundation, 1993.

Hilton, Jeanne M., and Virginia A. Haldeman. "Gender Differences in the Performance of Household Tasks by Adults and Children in Single-Parent and Two-Parent, Two Earner Families." *Journal of Family Issues* 12 (1991): 114–30.

Holmes, S. J., and L. N. Robbins. "The Role of Parental Disciplinary

Practices in the Development of Depression and Alcoholism." *Psychiatry* 51 (1988): 24–36.

Houser, R., et al. "A Systematic Behaviorally Based Technique for Resolving Conflicts Between Adolescents and Their Single Parents." *Child and Family Behavior Therapy* 15 (1993): 17–31.

Ishii-Kuntz, Masako. "Paternal Involvement and Perception Towards Fathers' Roles: A Comparison Between Japan and the United States." *Journal of Family Issues* 15 (1994): 30–48.

Kerin, S. F., and A. H. Beller. "Educational Attainment of Children From Single-Parent Families: Differences by Exposure, Gender and Race." *Demography* 25 (1988): 221–24.

King, V. "Nonresident Father Involvement and Child Well-Being: Can Dads Make a Difference." *Journal of Family Issues* 15 (1994): 78–96.

Ladd, J. *Out of the Madness.* New York: Warner Books, 1994.

McCall, Nathan. *Makes Me Wanna Holler.* New York: Random House, 1994.

McLanahan, Sara, and Karen Booth. "Mother-Only Families: Problems, Prospects, and Politics." *Journal of Marriage and the Family* 51 (1994): 557–80.

Melton, G. B., and F. D. Barry. "Neighbors Helping Neighbors: The Vision of the U.S. Advisory Board on Child Abuse and Neglect," in *Protecting Children From Abuse and Neglect: Foundation for a New National Strategy,* edited by Melton and Barry. New York: Guilford Press, 1994, 1–13.

Mott, Frank L. "When Is a Father Really Gone? Paternal-Child Contact in Father-Absent Homes." *Demography* 27 (1990): 499–515.

Phillips, Angela. *In Trouble With Boys.* New York: Basic Books, 1994.

Reich, Robert B. and Laura D'Andrea Tyson. "This Is No Way to Reward Work." *The Washington Post National Weekly Edition,* July 31–August 6, 1995.

"Restore the Floor: It's Time to Raise the Minimum Wage." AFL-CIO Report no. 86, October 1995.

Rice, F. P. *Human Development: A Life-Span Approach,* 2nd edition. Englewood Cliffs, N.J.: Prentice Hall, 1995.

Richards, Leslie, and Cynthia J. Schmiege. "Problems and Strengths of Single-Parent Families: Implications for Practice and Policy." *Family Relations* 42 (1993): 277–85.

Roberts, P. G. "Problem Support Orders: Problem With Enforcement," in *The Future of Children: Children and Divorce*, edited by R. H. Behrman, vol. 4, no. 1: 183–209. Los Altos, Calif.: The David and Lucile Packard Foundation, 1994.

Rosenfeld, Megan. "My Father's House Has Many Mansions." *Washington Post National Weekly Edition*, September 11–17, 1995.

Seltzer, Judith A., and Y. Brandreth. "What Fathers Say About Involvement With Children After Separation." *Journal of Family Issues* 15 (1994): 49–75.

Simons, Ronald L., et al. "The Impact of Mothers' Parenting, Involvement by Nonresidential Fathers, and Parental Conflict on the Adjustment of Adolescent Children." *Journal of Marriage and the Family* 56 (1994): 356–74.

Smith, Herbert L., and Morgan S. Philip. "Children's Closeness to Father as Reported by Mothers, Sons and Daughters: Evaluating Subjective Assessments With the Rasch Model." *Journal of Family Issues* 15 (1994): 3–29.

Staples, Robert. "Changes in Black Family Structure: The Conflict Between Family Ideology and Structural Conditions." *Journal of Marriage and the Family* vol. 37, no. 4 (November 1985): 1005–1012.

Starrels, Marjorie E. "Gender Differences in Parent-Child Relations." *Journal of Family Issues* 15 (1994): 148–65.

Straus, M. A., et al. *Behind Closed Doors: Violence in the American Family.* Garden City, New York: Anchor Books, 1994.

Tallmadge, J., and R. A. Barkley. "The Interactions of Hyperactive and Normal Boys with Their Mothers and Fathers." *Journal of Abnormal Child Psychology* 11 (1983): 565–79.

Teachman, J. D., and K. M. Paasch. "Financial Impact of Divorce on Children and Their Families," in *The Future of Children: Children and Divorce*, edited by R. H. Behrman, vol. 4, no. 1: 63–83. Los Altos, Calif.: The David and Lucile Packard Foundation, 1994.

Thomas, A. P. *Crime and the Sacking of America.* Washington, D.C.: Brassey's, 1994.

Todd, R. *Collect Your Child Support.* Brochure, National Legal Services, 1994.

U.S. Advisory Board on Child Abuse and Neglect. *Child Abuse and Neglect: Critical First Steps in Response to a National Emergency.* Washington, D.C.: U.S. Government Printing Office, 1990.

U.S. Government. "Financial Aid From the U.S. Department of Education." In *The Student Guide*, Washington, D.C.: U.S. Government Printing Office, 1995–96.

Wallerstein, J., and S. Blakeslee. *Second Chances: Men, Women, and Children a Decade After Divorce.* London: Grant McIntyre, 1990.

Wissow, L. S., and D. Roter. "Toward Effective Discussion of Discipline and Corporal Punishment During Primary Care Visits: Findings From Studies of Doctor-Patient Interaction." *Pediatrics* 94, no. 4 (1994): 587–93.

Wolfe, D. A. and A. McEachran. "Child Abuse and Neglect," in *Behavioral Assessment of Childhood Disorders*, edited by E. J. Mash and L. G. Terdal. New York: Guilford Press, 1988.

Wolfe, V. V., and D. A. Wolfe. "The Sexually Abused Child," in *Behavioral Assessment of Childhood Disorders*, edited by E. J. Mash and L. G. Terdal. New York: Guilford Press, 1988.

Index

◆ ◆ ◆ ◆ ◆